WHAT OTHERS
ARE SAYING

Dave Kahle has written a book that needs to be written, but will no doubt ruffle some feathers. Sometimes the truth about our history can hurt, but is also needed to cause change and rethink our strategy to equip the body of Christ for cultural influence. I encourage every church leader to read Is the Institutional Church Really The Church *to see how old paradigms and traditions often take us off the path God has for His people.*

—Os Hillman, author, TGIF Today
God Is First, and Change Agent

The title of this book, Is The Institutional Church Really The Church?, *is as necessary as it is challenging! It is necessary, because it touches on the heart of the Father for His Son's bride. It is challenging, because Dave is touching on the ultimate sacred cow. It is as if this is a question we dare not ask, because even the asking appears to be almost blasphemous. But ask it we must because if we don't ask good questions, we can never get down to the vital answers that we need to hear. For too long we have accepted the lame excuse, "But nothing is perfect." This book brings to mind Einstein's famous comment that it is unlikely that the thinking that gets us into a mess is likely to be up to the task of getting us out of the mess." We need new thinking, and this book is timely for it's challenge, and for it's prophetic willingness to point out some Biblical and practical ways forward. It really is time to stop going to church and instead start being the Church.*

—Dr. Tony Dale, Author and Businessman

Dave Kahle has authored a powerful and provocative work in this book. It will no doubt ruffle some feathers—but we must pay attention to the core things he addresses. Any company or organization that has lost its momentum and has seen its "market share" reduced must look itself squarely in the mirror and ask some tough questions. That is exactly what Kahle's book does. The "institutional church" is rapidly losing its impact in our culture, and we must ask ourselves if we should continue down our current path as followers of Jesus. What is the problem? What can and must be done? I encourage every follower of Christ desiring to make a radical impact on our culture read this book.

—Ray Hilbert, CEO Truth@Work

IS
THE
INSTITUTIONAL
CHURCH
REALLY
THE
CHURCH?

IS
THE
INSTITUTIONAL
CHURCH
REALLY
THE
CHURCH?

DAVE KAHLE

TATE PUBLISHING
AND ENTERPRISES, LLC

Published by Tate Publishing & Enterprises, LLC
127 E. Trade Center Terrace | Mustang, Oklahoma 73064 USA
1.888.361.9473 | www.tatepublishing.com

Tate Publishing is committed to excellence in the publishing industry. The company reflects the philosophy established by the founders, based on Psalm 68:11,
"The Lord gave the word and great was the company of those who published it."

Book design copyright © 2014 by Tate Publishing, LLC. All rights reserved.
Cover design by Nikolai Purpura
Interior design by Manolito Bastasa

Published in the United States of America

ISBN: 978-1-63122-694-6
1. Religion / Christian Church / General
2. Religion / Christian Ministry / General
14.04.22

ACKNOWLEDGMENT

There are some people who should be acknowledged. My wife, Coleen, has been my life-partner and co-sojourner through the experiences I share in this book. Tom Sudyk, my landlord and good friend, was a gadfly stimulating me to write it and prodding me along the way. Cheryl Cochran, my administrative assistant, read every word and proofed the entire text.

And of course, Jesus Christ, who gave his life for me and then lived with me through the entire course of events that lead to this book and who has prepared a place in heaven for me.

CONTENTS

FOREWORD

I'm sometimes asked how long it took to write a book. When it comes to this book, the answer is twofold.

In one sense, it took my entire life. I have experienced enough of life to be able to see the Lord's hand in my life, shaping the attitudes created in me, the events that impacted me, and the experiences that formed my perspectives. I can clearly see how the Lord shaped me to come to the point where I had to write this book. So in one sense, it took my entire life, being directed and formed by God, to give me the understandings, insights, and experiences that produced this work.

In a more specific sense, it took about two months of actual writing, from start to 95 percent finished. As any other author can attest, the last five percent takes forever, and may never be completely finished. There are always things you can improve in the manuscript.

I have written ten books prior to this one. This was, for me, a unique experience. I felt God's hand in the creation of it in ways that I have never experienced before. In my daily prayer times, I would receive thoughts for the book which I attribute to direction from God. In some cases, I would receive the exact set of words to use, and in others, I would understand a concept that I needed to add. Occasionally, a friend or acquaintance would mention something that appeared at just the right time to enlighten some aspect of the book.

While I expect to receive impassioned criticism from the religious establishment, I can honestly say that I am fully convinced that the Lord shaped my life with experiences and insights that positioned me uniquely to write this book. Then, He nudged and directed the actual writing. To a degree I've never known before, it's His book.

INTRODUCTION

Shortly after I came to Christ in my mid-twenties, I was struck with a question that has remained with me for decades. I saw the biblical account of the church that Christ instituted and noted the power which infused it. I saw that boldness of the early Christians and noted how rapidly the church spread, changing lives and upending culture as it expanded in every direction. It truly was changing the world as it expanded.

And then I looked at the church around me and wondered at its lack of power, its division, its political maneuvering and materialistic focus. I marveled at the majority of churchgoing Christians who seemed to be going through the motions. The churchgoers that I saw all around me seemed much more concerned with appearances and the outward trappings of Christianity—good Christians go to church three times a week—than they were living a transformed life. They just didn't seem to have the commitment, the motivation, the energy—the Holy Spirit—like the early Christians. And the "clergy"—everyone from the ritualistic priests of my Catholic upbringing, to the charismatic pastors of the evangelical movement—all seemed to be more interested in maintaining their positions and power as "the professional Christians." And I wondered, "Is the institutional church really the church?"

Of course, as a new Christian, who was I to question it? Surely these older and wiser people around me knew something that I didn't know. So I took their word for it, accepted their direction, and became more and more involved in the programs and working of the institutional church. I taught Bible school, made a dozen short-term mission trips, and eventually became an elder in the church. I spoke at church conferences, delivered sermons from the pulpit, and generally bought into one of the ubiquitous Christian paradigms: *The path to spiritual development is through active involvement with the institutional church.*

All this time, and for much of my adult life, I labored under the oppressive idea that I was a "second-class Christian." Because I did not have a seminary degree, I was never going to be as pleasing to the Lord as those who ran things.

As I grew more sure of myself, scripturally and spiritually, I began to occasionally voice my doubts and questions. Where is the power in the church? Where are the on-fire Christians? Why does what we do look so different than the biblical pattern?

The typical refrain was that the church is made up of imperfect people and is, therefore, not perfect. As one friend said to me, "It's not perfect, but it's the only thing we have."

That answer temporarily poured oil over the churning waters in my spirit. I reasoned, however, that the church of the New Testament was made up of imperfect people as well, and look at the difference. The reason was not, therefore, the people. Yet only a few people on the fringes ever stopped to question the establishment. Millions of churchgoers accepted the idea voiced by my friend without question.

I began to see the structure, the organization of the church as the culprit. Where did we get pastors, church boards, church buildings, etcetera anyway? I didn't see any of those in the church of the Bible. Could it be that we have, over time, imposed man-made structures on the pure church of the Bible, and in so doing robbed it of its power to transform people, culture, and the world?

When I became an elder of a small congregation, circumstances conspired to present me with an opportunity to test my ideas (see "What Happens When There Is No Pastor?" for the whole story). What would happen if we really tried to organize the church along biblical grounds?

In recent years, the Lord has given me a larger perspective. While the structure and organization of most of our churches is as far from the biblical pattern as black is from white, there are larger issues. We have created a man-made entity, which I call the institutional church system and supported it by the ubiquitous promotion of a series of paradigms whose power is so great that to even think of questioning them is to risk being treated with judgment and condemnation.

In this book, I share with you some of what I have learned, as I have studied the scriptures, reflected on my personal experiences, and beseeched the Lord for an answer to the question, "Is the institutional church really the church?"

† † †

****

I was recently interviewing a mature Christian business person for one of the spots in my Truth@Work Business Roundtables. "Tell me about your spiritual journey," I suggested. He launched into a description of his local church and the various roles he played in that institution. He was an usher, on this board or that board, served in this capacity, and was a part of these programs. Pretty impressive, except that nowhere did he mention Jesus Christ. His view of his spirituality was defined by the roles he played in his local congregation.

I could understand. Not so many years ago, I would have answered in exactly the same way. I suspect that most of the readers of this book would answer in a similar fashion as well. And that, unfortunately, is one of the saddest statements of our times. Instead of thinking of our spirituality as a relationship with Jesus Christ, we define it as involvement in the local church. The really sad part is that almost no one thinks it is sad!

Therein lies the crux of the issue which this manuscript confronts. We have allowed the institutional church system to define our spirituality in a superficial, man-made way, and the consequences have been enormous.

> *We have allowed the institutional church to define our spirituality in a superficial, man-made way, and the consequences have been enormous.*

See if this doesn't sound familiar.

You are a capable adult Christian. Maybe you are a business person. You have the ability to manage people, money, and projects. Maybe you have built a business from scratch, living through sleepless nights, and having more than one setback and failure. Or maybe you have excelled at the various positions you've held. You've learned a great deal about managing people, organizing systems, and getting things done. Those around you in the business world see you as a capable person of integrity.

In the big scheme of things, you are probably among the top twenty percent or so of people in your skills and accomplishments. Your energy, motivations, decisions, and ability to accept and handle risk have brought employment and opportunity to others.

In church, however, it's not quite that way. While you can easily lead a meeting in the business world, you are expected to sit in your pew and passively listen. Oh, you may be on a board, or even teach a class, but you have no doubt those are sort of secondary tasks, and they will never be of the stature or importance of the pastor.

There are times you wonder about the church. You are very hesitant to express some of those doubts, because, after all, it's the church. If you were to criticize or even question it, you'd be subject to disdain and be thought of as a bit odd, if not evil.

But still, you can't help but wonder from time to time. Is this really for what Jesus died? You know that sitting in a pew and listening to someone every week is hardly the best way to learn and actually promotes passivity. You'd never train your people for any kind of job using that methodology. But it's the church, and it seems like the principles you've learned and the wisdom you've gained just don't apply. Even when the pastor is the most fired up, exhorting you to action, you sense a flaw in that logic. He's still talking, and you're still in the pews listening. Less than a week later, you've forgotten what he talked about. Sometimes you wonder about the functionality of this. Isn't there a better way?

Generally, you try to fit in. You've volunteered for some program or service. They let you make coffee, be on a board, take up the collection. And you are happy to do it, because it serves the church. But you can't help but think this is hardly what the Lord created you to do. While there may be an occasional moment where you feel stirred by a song, or a particular portion of a sermon, for the most part, you can't wait to get out of church and back to work on Monday.

Believe me, I know how you feel. Those thoughts and doubts are very common. But very few business people have the courage to actually say what they are thinking. I see it in the looks in their eyes, the nods at a comment, the restlessness when the conversations drift to issues around the church and the pastor.

> *They let you make coffee, be on a board,*
> *take up the collection.*

I may be wrong, but I believe that 80 to 90 percent of the Christian business people in the world have thoughts and feelings that the church is something of a disappointment, not nearly what it should be.

Since you can't really criticize the church (it would be incredibly un-Christian), you internalize and think it must be you who is off center. So you keep it to yourself and continue to go through the motions.

It's for you that I am writing this book.

I am not so naive as to believe that most of the institutional Christians in this world will accept what I'm saying. Most will dismiss it outright. They are just too deeply embedded in the paradigms of the modern church to even think that it may not be just right. So if you're in that group, unwilling to even question some of the tenets of the institutional church system, read no further. This book will just harden your opinion and make you angry.

There is another larger group of people who sense that maybe there is something there, who feel what I just described, who have doubts, and who are thoughtful enough and sure enough of their own ability to think and make decisions that they will read and consider this book.

While I welcome your consideration, I have lived long enough to have few expectations for you. I understand that while you may intellectually agree with my observations, you are just too tied up in the institutional church to do anything about it. Your family is a founding member, your kids go to the youth group, and you're on the missions' board. You just can't see yourself extricating yourself from that web of entanglements. So you'll tell yourself that you can work inside the institution to change it.

And then, you'll be swallowed up by the enormous pressure and power of the breadth and depth of the cultural paradigms, which empower the institutional church system, and you'll be rendered spiritually impotent. Five years from now, nothing will have changed.

But there are maybe 20 percent of you who are open-minded enough to consider what I am saying and strong enough in your faith to do something about it.

For you, there is an exciting new future ahead. You no longer have to feel like a second-class Christian. You no longer have to feel that something is wrong with you for wondering about the church. You may be a part of one of the great movements of God in the world. You might just have a hand in saving Christianity in the Western world.

> *You may be a part of one of the great movements of God in the world. You might just have a hand in saving Christianity in the Western world.*

There are two other groups of people who will gain from reading this book. First are the disaffected Christians—people who have come to Christ but have some issue that keeps them from attending church. You don't feel comfortable in church, and you'd just rather not go. And frankly, you are tired of having to defend your position to the churchgoers in your life. For you, the message of this book is: "You're okay. Actually, you are right. There is something wrong, and you shouldn't go. It is them, not you. You can stop feeling guilty and like the odd one out among your churchgoing friends."

And the final group are those folks who are interested in Christ, believe in God, but have issues with the church that keep them from investigating Christ further. If churchgoing is part of what it means to be a Christian, you'll pass. For you, the message is this: "Please don't mistake church with Christianity. You can connect with Christ, transform your life, taste the 'peace which passes understanding,' and live a meaningful Christian life without ever going into a church building."

Both of these groups will get the message that you were right all along—it is them, not you. There are serious problems with the institutional church system, and you don't have to go to church to be a Christian.

Thinking About This Chapter

To what degree have you wondered about the difference between your local congregation and the church that you see in the Bible?

To what extent have you felt like you were a second-class Christian because you are not a member of the "clergy"?

Could it be that some of your beliefs about the church may be incorrect?

To what degree do you think of your Christianity in terms of your involvement with the programs of the church?

To what extent are your spiritual gifts unleashed and expressed in your local congregation?

Have you have ever felt like you just didn't fit in your local congregation?

WE'VE LOST
THE CULTURE

In the early 1960s, this country could be character-
ized as being predominantly Christian.

Over the last fifty years, in the space of one or
two generations, we have lost the culture. This is an epic
failure, akin to the ancient Israelites giving up the worship of Jehovah and turning to idols. Our culture has
done exactly that. We have removed God from a central position in our culture and, in His place, have substituted the idols of our times. Greed, sex, power, and
secular humanism have replaced Christ as the bedrock
of our culture.

It's an incredible turn of events. Here we were, the
richest, most prosperous, most Christian nation on
earth, founded on Christian principles by Godly men,
with a rich culture of God in our schools, in our media,
and in our government. Then, in the space of one or two
generations, we have lost it.

> *Here we were, the richest, most prosperous, most Christian nation on earth, founded on Christian principles by godly men, with a rich culture of God in our schools, in our media, and in our government. Then, in the space of one or two generations, we have lost it.*

If we were in biblical times, the last fifty years and the incredible loss of this country would warrant several chapters in an Old Testament book. The change is so epic, the loss so devastating, that it is almost inconceivable.

The election of 2012 was the tipping point. The results were a shock to many evangelical Christians, who, mostly of conservative political persuasion, saw the election as an opportunity to turn the country around. They were stunned with the outcome. They see the reelection of Barack Obama as an incomprehensible political mistake.

From my perspective, as a nation, we got the government we wanted. The American people had been leaving the conservative Christian viewpoint all along. The election was a symptom—an expression of a greater trend. And that trend was and is the de-Christianization of this country.

There is something seriously wrong with Western Christianity—what I call the institutional church system—to have allowed (maybe even caused) this cataclysmic shift.

And we are at fault. We have allowed the institutional church system to reign, and we've accepted the flaws and gone on about our ways.

Let me define my terms. It is important to note the difference between the institutional church and the larger, universal church—the church for which Christ died. The universal church is made up of every Christian everywhere around the world. The Greek word that is used to denote the church in the New Testament is *Ekklesia*, and it means, "the called out." In the New Testament, no one *went* to church. They *were* the church.

No one *joins* the church. Christ *adds* them to it. In Acts 3:47, as the writer describes the early days of the church, he says, "And the Lord *added* to their number daily those who were being saved."

There are no denominations in the church of the Bible. In fact, following after a person or that person's teaching is expressly condemned in the New Testament.

> I appeal to you, brothers and sisters, in the name of our Lord Jesus Christ, that all of you agree with one another in what you say and that there be no divisions among you, but that you be perfectly united in mind and thought. My brothers and sisters, some from Chloe's household have informed me that there are quarrels among you. What I mean is this: One of you says, "I follow Paul"; another, "I follow Apollos"; another, "I follow Cephas"; still another, "I follow Christ."
>
> Is Christ divided? Was Paul crucified for you? Were you baptized in the name of Paul?
>
> (1 Corinthians 1:10–13)

So we have the universal church for which Christ died, made up of every Christian, headed by Christ, and lead by the Holy Spirit. Inside of that is the institutional western church. It's the institutional church system—that portion of the universal church—which we commonly call church.

In this book, the term "institutional church" and more precisely the "institutional church system" refers to what has been traditionally the most common expression of Christianity in western civilization—the local congregation, headed by a professional pastor, connected to a church building, and organized around Sunday morning worship services. Those are the core elements. But the term refers to the entire body of institutions and bureaucracies which have arisen to support that. It includes the seminaries that produce trained pastors, the denominations and all of their various levels of organization and bureaucracies, and the parachurch organizations which provide services to those seminaries, denominations, and congregations.

The Institutional church system is the entire body of institutions and bureaucracies which have arisen to support the local paid pastor and church building. It includes the seminaries which produce trained pastors, the denominations and all of their various levels of organization and bureaucracies, and the para-church organizations which provide services to those seminaries, denominations and congregations.

The institutional church system is all of that together. As a matter of convenience, I'll be using the abbreviation ICS to denote the institutional church system in the balance of this manuscript.

Something is very wrong. Consider this. According to Os Hillman, citing research from George Barna, in his book *Faith & Work*,

> Although churches in the US have spent more than $530 billion dollars on ministry activities since 1980, the proportion of adults who are born again has remained virtually the same during the last 15 years.[1]

Stop for a minute, and consider that. You know the value of investment and the need to get a return on it. You understand performance and productivity. Now, if you were part of an organization that had spent $530 billion dollars, with no noticeable return, no measurable growth, wouldn't you question that?

Of course you would. You would have put that organization out of its misery years ago. What sane person would allow that situation to continue if you had any influence over it?

By any common sense measure, something is very wrong.

I understand that it is difficult to take that big picture perspective. We look at the church from our individual perspectives and our local congregation. Our church may be growing, for example. Or it may have a great youth group or inspiring music or a really good marriage enrichment series. From our individual perspective, things look upbeat. What could be wrong?

Step back for a moment and take a bigger picture point of view. Let's say things are growing and promising in your congregation at the moment. Let's say that is true for 30 percent of the local congregations in this country. Now, fold those in with the others, add in the seminaries and institutional church-oriented parachurch ministries, and look at the big picture. Look at the church in this country. Is your church growing because people are leaving other congregations to come to yours? Are we just shuffling around the same people, from one congregation to another? The ICS, the entire entity made up of tens of thousands of congregations and all that is associated with it, is the issue.

> *The big picture is $530 billion and no growth.*
> *Something is very wrong.*

> *We've spent $530 billion, we haven't grown a*
> *percentage point, and we've lost the culture. Clearly,*
> *something is terribly wrong.*
> *Shouldn't we stop and question what we are doing?*

Let's look a little closer at the culture.

John Enlow's book *The Seven Mountain Prophecy* provides a useful way to analyze the extent to which we have lost the culture. In it, he describes the "seven mountains" of culture.[2] Let's look at each to determine the depth and breadth of the loss.

We've lost the mountain of celebration. That's the name for the element of society which contains what we may more commonly call arts and entertainment. In 2012, the top three best-selling books of the year were the pornographic *Fifty Shades of Grey Series*, followed by a series by the author of *Hunger Games*, where teenagers are pitted against each other in a futuristic gladiator contest.[3]

Speaking of pornography, it is now so pervasive in our society that it is available with one or two clicks from everyone's computer, tablet, or smart phone. The trend among teens and preteen girls is to send naked pictures of themselves to their boyfriends, a practice known as sexting. It seems that every celebrity has a sex tape of themselves making the rounds on the Internet. It is almost like a rite of passage in Hollywood.

Christians are routinely portrayed in mainstream movies and TV shows as buffoons. The national media, from the highly-sexualized sitcoms to the late-night talk show hosts, all project an attitude that Christians are a simple-minded, highly prejudiced underclass.

Video games, those things with which preteens and teens spend hours, are increasingly violent. The most popular games all seem to involve stealing cars, shooting bad guys, or slicing up monsters. Our children become calloused to violence by the countless hours tuned in to these fantasies. Then, some of them go out and kill children and other teens before turning their violence on themselves. Mass killings by teenagers seem to be a growing trend, and our schools are more violent and less safe than the streets.[4]

Let's try to be objective about this. Suppose a visitor from outer space arrived here, with the mission to observe the culture and report back on its major trends and influences. This alien visitor had no preconceived notions and no background to color his observations.

Our alien visitor, looking objectively at the output of our TV, movies, and news stations would make the observation that Christianity has no serious role in any of this and was, in fact, a minor subculture of underclass simpletons.

In the mountain of "families" living together outside of marriage is now the expectation for young couples. According to one source, "The number of cohabitating unmarried couples increased by 88 percent between 1990 and 2007."[5] Now, 48 percent of women cohabite with a man as their "first union."[6] Traditional marriage is on the outs. One estimate puts the likelihood of divorce at between 50 percent and 74 percent.[7] The president of the United States is now advocating gay marriage, and a number of states have approved it. According to researcher David Kinnaman, writing in *unChristian*,

> Currently more than one-third of children born in the United States are born to unmarried mothers; in 1960 the ratio was just one out of twenty births. In some American metropolitan areas, as many as two-thirds of all infants are born to unmarried women.[8]

In the world of education, our schools, which were originally designed to promote the reading and studying of the Bible, have pretty much swept any vestiges of Christianity from the curriculums and practices and replaced it with the religion of secular humanism. Jesus said, "I am the way, the truth and the life. No one comes to the Father except through me." (John 14:6). In the place of this foundational cornerstone of Christianity, our schools now promote diversity.

According to Michael J. Metarko, writing in *Indoctrination,*

> With 90 percent of Christians still sending their children into this statist educational system, I need to be brutally direct. According to current research, if you send your child to public school, you WILL most likely lose your child to the secular humanistic worldview. In two reports to the Southern Baptist Convention, T.C. Pinckney found that 70–88 percent of evangelical teens will leave the faith within two years of graduating from high school.[11] The fatal combination of secular education and the lack of true biblical discipleship is reflected in separate studies by the Barna Group and Britt Beemer of America's Research Group. They found that one-third of twenty-somethings who were churched as teens have disengaged spiritually. Over "60 percent of the children that grow up in our churches will leave them as they reach the threshold of young adulthood."[12]

> We are losing more children much younger
> than previously thought: 83 percent of those
> surveyed started doubting the Bible in middle
> school and high school.[9]

In the sphere of politics, our political parties have become so extreme that it appears they rarely speak to one another, compromise rarely happens, and the federal government is on a path to replace the providential role of God and Christian benevolence. The federal deficit is the largest in human history. As the political parties gather more and more power to themselves in Washington, DC, the stage is being set for a dictator to seize total political power. If our current trends continue, I expect to see the end of democracy in the United States within twenty years and a dictator takes its place.

More people now receive food stamps than at any other time in history. According to Mitt Romney's often quoted comment, 47 percent of the population are now dependent upon the federal government for at least a portion of their livelihood. The Christian concept of "The one who is unwilling to work shall not eat" (2 Thessalonians 3:10) has been smothered in the tidal wave of endless unemployment benefits, Medicaid, food stamps, and government handouts of countless varieties.

Our alien observer, reporting back to his supervisors on his observations of American culture, would not use the word "Christian" to describe any element of it. It just would not be a significant enough factor to even be noticed by the objective outside observer.

In one generation, we've lost the culture.

We've spent $530 billion, we haven't grown a percentage point, and we've lost the culture. Clearly, something is terribly wrong. Shouldn't we question this?

> *Something is terribly wrong. It's time we asked some questions. More of the same is not the solution.*

Thinking About This Chapter

To what extent are you comfortable with the direction in which the culture is moving?

To what extent do you believe that the culture today is less Christian than it was when you were growing up?

How do you explain the fact that we have spent $530 billion on "church" and not increased the percentage of Christians in the country by even one percent?

To what degree is it possible that your children or grandchildren could be part of the 60 to 80% who leave the church?

Doesn't it seem like something is very wrong?

AND THAT'S NOT ALL

There are other consequences—huge, spiritual consequences.

WE ARE LOSING OUR CHILDREN

They are leaving the church in droves. In his book *You Lost Me*, pollster David Kinnaman, president of the Barna Group, shares research which indicates that 43 percent of teenagers who are raised in the church leave it by the time they are thirty. He estimates the current number at about eight million. Interestingly, Kinnaman has discovered that "most young Christians are struggling less with their faith in Christ than with their experience of church."[10]

In other words, it is not Christ who turns them off and drives them away, it's the church.

All that sounds pretty academic until it's your child. One of my Truth@Work members recently shared the anguish and guilt he felt when his twenty-year-old came home from college and announced that he no longer considered himself to be a Christian. And this after a typical upbringing in an institutional church—

youth groups, Bible classes, junior church, youth camps, and attendance multiple times a week. Here's a godly Christian man who did everything the ICS told him to do and had his children in every program they offered, and it still wasn't good enough.

Does that sound like a church empowered by the Holy Spirit?

My Truth@Work member's story is hardly unique. Almost every mature Christian I know has a similar story to tell.

For about half of our young people, all that church just doesn't work. In fact, it has the opposite impact. It drives them away.

But it's even worse than that. Looking at teens who have been converted to Christ, Kinnaman, quoting Barna Group research, discovered that:

> Eight out of ten students participate in church during their teenage years, but most of them will take a permanent detour from active faith at some point soon after they get their driver's licenses. That's right: only two out of ten of those celebrated teenage converts maintain Christian belief and practice between their teens and the end of their twenties. The vast majority will cross over to the other side: pronouncing Christianity boring, irrelevant, and out of touch.[11]

Doesn't that cause you to stop and question? We spend $530 billion dollars and lots of time and effort, and we only keep somewhere between 20 percent to 50 percent of our children. Shouldn't we be a little better at it than that?

Let's make this personal. If you want your children to grow up as committed Christians, you had better consider pulling them out of the institutional church system because it's likely to drive them away.

Just because it is the church doesn't mean that we should abandon all common sense. Someone should at least ask the question. Doesn't it seem that there is something horribly wrong here?

"But who knows God's will," some of you will say. "Maybe it is his will that they drop out. Maybe they will come back later. And regarding the culture, maybe that isn't a bad thing. Maybe it's God's will that it go the other way. How are we to know?"

I understand that thought process. Maybe, in the big picture of his eternal plan, all this is as it should be. Just like the Israelites forsaking God and worshipping the idols of the people around them. Maybe, in the big picture, that was God's will. He just didn't seem too happy about it though.

It remains possible for the apologist of the established church to rationalize the failures of the church with that mindset. There is, however, one clear consequence of the ICS that no one can dismiss. Division.

DIVISION

Let's put this in perspective. God wants unity among his people. In his last recorded prayer, Jesus prays for unity.

> My prayer is not for them alone. I pray also for those who will believe in me through their message, that all of them may be one, Father, just as you are in me and I am in you. May they also be in us so that the world may believe that you have sent me. I have given them the glory that you gave me, that they may be one as we are one—I in them and you in me—so that they may be brought to complete unity. Then the world will know that you sent me and have loved them even as you have loved me.

(John 17:20–23)

He passionately prays for unity among his people, acknowledging that unity among Christians is a sign to the world that we are of Christ. By implication, a lack of unity indicates the opposite.

In spite of his prayer, we have created a system with over forty thousand denominations, each finding some way to separate itself from the others. Not only that, but many congregations have spilt even further, some multiple times.

To the objective observer, this division would be the first thing he/she would notice. "Why is there a church on this corner and a different one up the road?" You can see him puzzling as he asks the question.

"Just minor differences," the establishment apologist would remark. "At the heart, we all believe the same thing."

Wasn't that just exactly the same situation that Paul confronted in the Corinthian church? In 1 Corinthians 10:

> I appeal to you, brothers and sisters, in the name of our Lord Jesus Christ, that all of you agree with one another in what you say and that there be no divisions among you, but that you be perfectly united in mind and thought. My brothers and sisters, some from Chloe's household have informed me that there are quarrels among you. What I mean is this: One of you says, "I follow Paul"; another, "I follow Apollos"; another, "I follow Cephas"; still another, "I follow Christ.
>
> Is Christ divided? Was Paul crucified for you? Were you baptized in the name of Paul? I thank God that I did not baptize any of you except Crispus and Gaius, so no one can say that you were baptized in my name. (Yes, I also baptized the household of Stephanas; beyond that, I don't remember if I baptized anyone else.) For Christ did not send me to baptize, but to preach the gospel—not with wisdom and eloquence, lest the cross of Christ be emptied of its power.

So Paul confronts and condemns the very situation we have created in this time. Like denominational Christians of every sort, those Corinthians all believed basically the same thing. But they followed after different leaders, dividing themselves into camps. Sort of the apostolic times version of denominations and church splits. It was not okay then, and it is not okay today.

Make no mistake. The denominations and church splits are not God's will. They are sin. And yet, we continue to make excuses for it. Paul even foretells the consequence. If you preach with "wisdom and eloquence, the cross of Christ will be emptied of its power."

Stop and consider that verse. You have probably never heard a sermon on it. Paul, in talking about division in the church, chose that subject to make a statement that you will never see discussed from the pulpit: When you emphasize "wisdom and eloquence, you empty the cross of its power."

Wow. What do we admire most in our pastors? Wisdom and eloquence. What causes one congregation to grow? The wisdom and eloquence of its pastor. What do seminaries aspire to instill in their students? Isn't wisdom and eloquence up high on the list?

Could it be that we have this twisted all around?

Maybe that's why we have squandered 530 billion dollars, lost the culture, not gained one percentage point in converts, divided into forty thousand different camps, and continually lose up to 80 percent of our children.

But that's not all.

WE CONDONE (AND PROMOTE) MEDIOCRE CHRISTIANITY

Put the rhetoric aside. Don't look at what the ICS says, look at what the ICS does. It assembles large groups of people into a big room, entertains them for twenty to thirty minutes, and then someone preaches to them for another thirty to forty-five minutes in a worship service. A few people are active, and the vast majority are passive.

That is an environment that promotes superficial commitment. It is possible that someone can come in, sit in on the worship service every Sunday for years, and never speak to anyone, never grow one iota spiritually, and yet think that he/she was a good Christian. After all, he did what the ICS wanted him to do.

The larger the congregation, the easier it is to be anonymous and mediocre. It's not a difficult concept. As a professional speaker, I can tell you that when the audience is three hundred or five hundred or more, people can come and go without hardly being noticed, and it is easy for people to carry on side conversations, play on their computer, and daydream. When the audience is ten to twenty, it's almost impossible to do those things.

The environment promotes superficial commitment. Is it any wonder that Christianity has devolved to a ritual that only really transforms a small portion of the congregation? Is it any wonder that the vast majority of Christians are superficial, thinking that going to church is sufficient?

After all, didn't Paul say that when you emphasize "wisdom and eloquence," you "empty the cross of its power"?

We Have Failed to Transform the Lives of Christians

"But," some of you are thinking. "We have to go to church. How else will we be 'fed'? If we didn't have pastors teaching us, how would we grow?"

I understand this point of view. There was a time when I believed it too. The problem is, for the most part, Christians in the ICS don't grow. Christianity does not impact their lives in any observable way.

Now, I understand that you may have grown as a Christian. You may have a small group of friends or churchgoing colleagues who have also matured spiritually. So your perspective is formed by those closest around you. Granted that there are, in every congregation, a small percentage of people who are impacted and transformed by Christ.

However, you are the exception, not the rule. I would submit that you have grown spiritually in spite of, not because of, your involvement in the ICS. The reality is that the ICS absolutely fails to impact the lives of the vast majority of churchgoers.

Don't take my word for it. Here's pollster David Kinnaman's conclusions:

> In virtually every study we conduct, representing thousands of interviews every year, bornagain Christians fail to display much attitudinal or behavioral evidence of transformed lives. For instance, based on a study released in 2007, we found that most of the lifestyle activities of

born-again Christians were statistically equivalent to those of non-born-agains. When asked to identify their activities over the last thirty days, born-again believers were just as likely to bet or gamble, to visit a pornographic web site, to take something that did not belong to them, to consult a medium or psychic, to physically fight or abuse someone, to have consumed enough alcohol to be considered legally drunk, to have used an illegal, non-prescription drug, to have said something to someone that was not true, to have gotten back at someone for something he or she did, and to have said mean things behind another person's back. No difference.[12]

In drilling down deeper into this phenomena, Kinnaman examined sexual attitudes:

> One study we conducted examined American's engagement in some type of sexually inappropriate behavior, including looking at online pornography, viewing sexually explicit magazines or movies, or having an intimate sexual encounter outside of marriage. In all, we found that 30 percent of born-again Christians admitted to at least one of these activities in the past 30 days, compared to 35 percent of other Americans. In statistical and practical terms, this means the two groups are essentially no different from each other.[13]

While the Barna Group's research results are one thing, I believe that each of us have a personal observation that supports his conclusions. We all know people who claim to be "born-again," attend the worship services at the ICS with regularity and yet live lives that fail to show any kind of Christ influence.

As an employer, I must confess that I'm a little hesitant to hire proclaimed "Christians." While there are lots of exceptions, my experience has been that they don't have the same sense of personal responsibility that I expect in an employee.

In my work as a Truth@Work chapter president, I am continually amazed at the number of supposedly mature Christian churchgoers who, after a very cordial meeting of an hour or so, don't feel any need to answer an email or accept a phone call.

And while I get it that we are all sinners, saved by grace, one purpose of grace and Christ's presence in the lives of his followers is to transform those lives. If we continue for decades to preach at people and see no measurable impact in their lives, we have to question what we are doing, don't we?

If we can't even impact the lives of our churchgoers, is it any wonder that we haven't impacted the culture?

Of course, this should come as no surprise to the serious Bible scholar. Paul did say that when we focus on "wisdom and eloquence," we "empty the cross of its power."

THE LOST TURNED OFF

There is a church near my house that celebrates when someone comes to Christ by lighting a candle on the stage. It seems like the candle is lit about half the time. Being very generous, let's say the church celebrates one hundred converts a year or so.

Everyone feels good about that. Look at the good work they are doing. Except…

There are about five thousand people who attend that church. While every soul is precious, I have to wonder about that. I would think that a good portion of those new Christians are children who are raised in the church. According to David Kinnaman, 43 percent of them will leave by the time they are thirty. The new converts may not even make up for those who leave, die, and opt out of Christianity.

So as this one particular institutional church celebrates bringing a small number of people to Christ, it isn't anything like the early church, which penetrated the entire world in just a few hundred years.

One of the things that I have learned is to look at the spaces between the lines, the blanks on a résumé, and the things that are meaningful by their omission. While one hundred new converts is worth celebrating, as is just one new convert, I have to question how many should have been there but weren't. How many non-Christians have you met who have some objection to the church? They may believe in God, or even in Christ, but have never given themselves to him because of something about the church. You've heard it, I'm sure.

It seems like the majority of those who reject Christ, when pressed as to why, uncover a disenchantment with some aspect of the church. Churchgoers are hypocrites, or judgmental, and the disenchanted just don't fit into the culture of the culture. In other words, at the heart of things, it's not Christ they reject, it's their perception of church—the institutional church system. How many millions could be brought to Christ, if we disengage church attendance from the equation? Would we open the doors of Christianity if we separated the ICS from Christianity?

While every institutional church celebrates converts, I have never heard of one who measured the number of people who were turned off by their worship services. No one is standing at the back door counting the number of people who come once or twice and never again.

NOT ONLY ARE WE DOING A POOR JOB OF BRINGING THE LOST TO CHRIST, BUT WE ARE ACTUALLY DOING THE OPPOSITE—WE ARE CAUSING MORE HARM THAN GOOD!

I know that seems like an outlandish comment but stop a minute and consider the research. It seems that, by promoting a superficial brand of Christianity, we are inoculating the population from committing to Christ.

In his book *unChristian*, David Tinnaman shares some remarkable data.

> In America the vast majority of people (even outsiders) are exposed to the message of Christianity many times throughout their lives—in churches, via media, through their friendships, and so on. For instance, among non-Christian

ages sixteen to twenty-nine—that is, atheists, agnostics, those undecided about their faith, and individuals affiliated with other faiths—more than four out of every five have gone to a Christian church at some time in their life (82 percent). Most of these attended for at least three months.[14]

Let's consider this. Based on research, most of those outside of the Church—82 percent of the non-Christians between the ages of sixteen to twenty-nine—have attended a Christian church at some time in their lives! Halleluiah! We are getting them into the churches! That's an incredible statistic.

The problem is that what happens there so turns them off that they are lost to Christianity for the rest of their lives.

It's like we are vaccinating them from ever considering Christ again. A vaccination is made from dead and powerless organisms, that when injected into our body prevents us from contacting the real thing. That's exactly what we are doing to the lost around us. We bring them into our churches, and they become exposed to the powerless, superficial, pastor-centric system that so turns them off, they become immune to the real power of Christ.

> Most outsiders have grown up around Christians; many have given the "Jesus thing" a thorough test drive; a majority have tried churches and found them desperately lacking relevance.[15]

This is something to which no one pays attention. Everyone's attention is on the front of the sanctuary, where the visible one or two people ask for prayer. No one is watching those who are visiting and deciding that they don't want any part of this.

Given the sobering message of this research, shouldn't we at least ask the question? Doesn't it look like the institutional church system does more harm than good?

LET'S SUMMARIZE

In the last two generations, we have seen the culture change from predominately Christian to anti-Christian. We condone and promote mediocre, superficial Christianity that does not transform the lives of its adherents. We have spent 530 billion dollars and not grown one percentage point. We turn off and drive away somewhere between 50 and 82 percent of our children. We have split into forty thousand denominations and continue to see congregations split. We put barriers in the way of people who may be interested in Christ and may, in fact, inoculate people from ever committing their lives to Christ.

Ladies and gentlemen, something is terribly wrong. It's time we asked some questions. More of the same is not the solution. The solution is bigger than adding video to the sermon and a coffee shop in the foyer.

Something is terribly wrong. It's time we asked some questions. More of the same is not the solution.

THINKING ABOUT THIS CHAPTER

How many people do you know who have seen their children or grandchildren raised in the church and leave it?

Have you ever compared the current state of division in the church with Jesus's prayer in John 17:20–23?

How do you account for the superficial character of most Christians today, when compared to the passionate devotion of the early Christians?

To what degree do you know Christians whose lives do not show evidence of transformation?

To what degree have you been focused on the small number of successes that the church has and, at the same time, not aware of the large number of people it has been turning off?

To what extent have you been aware of the inoculation function of the church—that we actually inoculate people from ever being interested in Christ again?

To what extent does it seem like something is terribly wrong?

IT'S OUR FAULT

We have lost the culture. We have spent 530 billion dollars and not grown one percentage point. We turn off and drive away half our children. We have split into forty thousand denominations and continue to see congregations split. We condone and promote mediocre, superficial Christianity. We put barriers in the way of people who may be interested in Christ. And it's our fault.

We have built a flawed system. We have supported that system with a series of cultural paradigms so powerful that to even question those paradigms is to be viewed as a heretic and become the subject of wrath from the established religious powers. We have blinded ourselves to the fundamental flaws in the system.

Specifically, we have allowed the ICS to delude us into a misconception of what Christianity is and what it means to be a Christian. We've spent a lot of our time on the wrong things, with our attention focused in the wrong places. As a result, we have lost the culture.

First, a little perspective.

We all have deep-seated beliefs that impact our view of the world. These beliefs have formed in us over a period of many years, beginning with our childhood and continuing until now. They are often so deep within us that we are not consciously aware of them. Yet because they define how we see the world, these deep-seated beliefs shape our attitudes, impact our emotions, shape our thoughts, and determine our behaviors. For want of a better word, let's call them paradigms.

These paradigms impact everything we do and can cause individuals, as well as entire groups of people, to act in certain ways. For example, in Christopher Columbus's day, most of the world thought the earth was flat. This paradigm meant that they would not sail to the horizon because they did not want to fall off the earth. The vast majority of people never questioned the fact that the earth was flat. They went about their lives operating on this mistaken belief about the nature of the world.

It took someone like Columbus to question that paradigm and act differently. Prior to his journey, people were held back by their beliefs—this paradigm—not by the reality of the situation.

The same is true for all of us. Our paradigms impact everything we do, because they color our perceptions of what the world is really like. These deep-seated beliefs help us to make sense out of the world around us. Without them, we'd be unable to function.

However, we are always at risk of nurturing paradigms, which incorrectly interpret the world and cause us to act in ways that are not positive. Here's an example from my life. At one time, my wife and I were visiting in the South African township of Soweto, which is the big African township that borders Johannesburg. On the day we were visiting, the elementary children were on strike—refusing to go to school. As strange as that sounds, it wasn't the punch line.

Why were they on strike? Because they were objecting to being graded as individuals. Their position was, either the whole class passes or the whole class fails. To grade people as individuals would be to allow some people to rise above the others, and that violated their deeply held paradigm about community and what it means to be a tribe.

For us in western culture, that appears to be a paradigm, which has worked against the development of that community and maybe a part of the reason why that entire continent is thought of as "developing," even though its civilizations are ancient.

While I'm not going to argue the point, note that this group of children shared a paradigm many would say works against their development and prosperity. My point is this: Our paradigms can be erroneous, leading us to misspent energy and errant actions.

I believe the modern institutional church system has been supported and held in place by a set of erroneous paradigms of this nature.

> *The modern institutional church system has been supported and held in place by a set of paradigms of this nature.*

I've recently discovered an image that helps me to understand. Imagine you have a large wooden box, which is open on one side. The inside of the box is lined with shiny aluminum foil. Inside the box is a powerful light in the shape of a globe. Now imagine you place that box in a dark room and turn on the light. It would allow a powerful beam of light to shine from the open side, illuminating everything around it.

That's sort of like us and the Holy Spirit. We're the box that contains the light, and the Holy Spirit is the

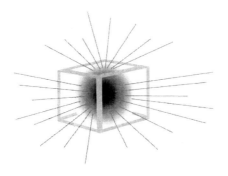

light shining out from us, illuminating a dark world.

Now, take a screen, like the kind that we use on windows and doors to keep the bugs out. Nail that screen over the open side of the box.

What will be the effect? The screen will have slightly cut down on the amount of light shining out of the box. The light will still be there, just as powerful as ever, but the screen will have hindered its impact on the world outside of the box. And what would happen if you would then nail layer after layer of screens on that open side of the box? With each succeeding layer, you would have hindered a little bit more of the light until the light has been totally contained.

Our errant paradigms are like those screens nailed to the opening. We have the Holy Spirit in his full expression, just as the early Christians did, but we have hindered the expression and power of the Holy Spirit by nailing layer after layer of incorrect paradigms over the power of the Holy Spirit. Not one of them is sufficient to totally hinder the power of the Spirit, but the sum total of all of them does the job.

We can look at people groups scattered around the world and marvel at the things that some believe. We can see how their lives are shaped for both good as well as evil by their belief systems. Whole countries exist in which citizens' lives are shaped by the power of false religious beliefs. *National Geographic* regularly brings us views of people who lives are controlled by the dictates of the culture in which they are raised. Culture—the combination of beliefs, values, and practices, which are taught and supported by the community—is one of the most powerful and pervasive forces in our lives.

Yet while we can look at others and see some of the false beliefs in their lives, it's very difficult to see them in our own. Since we, too, are raised to accept certain beliefs, these beliefs gradually embed themselves into the core of our minds, dictating the quality of our lives, while we often remain blissfully unaware of their impact.

That is exactly the case in which we find ourselves today. There are certain culturally supported beliefs that are widespread throughout the modern institutional church. It doesn't matter what the particular flavor of the church is, its denominational affiliation or its position on the charismatic/Pentecostal/conservative spectrum. It doesn't matter if it's in the USA or any other Western country. Regardless of these differences, almost every congregation holds these beliefs and adheres to these practices.

Not only are these practices pervasive, they're also so deeply held that virtually no one questions them. Created and supported by the culture, they have achieved the status of unquestioned truth. To even question them makes your Christianity suspect. Go into any institutional church anywhere in the Western world or one of the clones created by the western missionary effort, try advocating a position contrary to these beliefs, and you'll be asked to leave immediately. They are so fundamental that few churches can stand to have them violated. To do so threatens the very core of the church. These fundamental paradigms are the practical foundations of the modern institutional church system.

But are they right? Are they scriptural? Are they part of God's plan for his church? Or are they culturally induced paradigms that have developed out of man's thoughts and are contrary to God's expressed directions?

Few people have ever questioned them.

Before I examine some of them, let's consider one more concept. Throughout history, there has often been a conflict between practices that seemed good to mankind, and those practices that were given by God. Typically, God has instituted some practice among men, but mankind has decided to change things to some other order because it seemed good to them.

One example is the cry of the Israelite people for a king. The story is told in I Samuel 8. God had ordained the system of judges and prophets to organize and administer his nation. But the Israelites looked around them at neighboring nations and saw that they had kings. They too wanted a king. It seemed good to them. A king could unify the people, bring organization to their country, be a rallying point for the people, lead them in battle, and make them just like the other nations around them. All good reasons to want a king. All reasonable, valid things. Having a king seemed like a good thing.

But God had a better practice. A simpler, more direct way of organizing his people that kept Him in the forefront. No king standing in the middle between God and his people.

However, He eventually gave them what they asked for. He said to Samuel, "It is not you they have rejected as their king, it is me" (1 Samuel 8:7). Saul was then appointed the first of a line of Israelite kings. And some good came out of that. The Israelites defeated their enemies in battle, power was consolidated around the king, and, eventually, under Solomon, the Israelite nation achieved great prosperity and influence. These were all good things from man's perspective.

However, the net result was devastating. The Israelite people lost their reliance on prophets and judges and thus moved further from God. Their focus often strayed from the things of God to the political maneuvering of the royalty. Power struggles and moral corruption became commonplace. The kings led the Israelites into idolatry on numerous occasions. And the institution of the rule of kings led to the division of the Israelite people into two kingdoms and the eventual loss of the ten tribes.

How much better would their lives have been if they had only stuck to God's simple plan and practices for them rather than following their own ideas of what was good?

This conflict between God's simple practices and man's "improved" vision of what is good is a theme that crops up continually in the Bible. God even told us about it in so many words.

> "For my thoughts are not your thoughts, neither are your ways my ways," declares the Lord."
>
> (Isaiah 55:8)

It began with Adam and Eve and continued throughout the Bible. It was, in part, what Jesus condemned the Pharisees for and certainly added to the motivation of those who crucified him. Even in the last book of the Bible, *Revelation*, Jesus condemns the Nicolaitans for following practices that they considered to be good instead of God's simple practices that are best for His church.[16]

This constant conflict between God's simple practices for his people and our ever-evolving image of what is good is one of the basic themes of the Bible.

It's my view that these culturally-supported, unquestioned paradigms and practices of the modern church fall into this same category. Rather than following God's simple plan and practices for His people, church leaders have instead developed practices, which they see as good. These paradigms have become the culture at our churches. And these good things crowd out and substitute for God's best with devastating consequences.

We have lost the culture. We haven't grown a bit. We drive our children away. We condone mediocrity. We put barriers in the way of people who may be interested in Christ. It's our fault. We allowed ourselves to believe some false paradigms.

> *We have lost the culture. We haven't grown a bit. We drive our children away. We condone mediocrity. We put barriers in the way of the lost. It's our fault. We allowed ourselves to believe some false paradigms.*

What are these paradigms and practices? These unquestioned myths that seem good to us but that deviate from God's best? These culturally supported practices?

That's the next chapter.

Thinking About This Chapter

To what extent is it possible that you could believe some paradigms regarding Christianity and the church that are wrong?

Is it possible that some of our beliefs about the church are actually hindering the work of the spirit?

In what way is Israel's quest for a king like our expectation of today's church?

Could it be possible that God's views of the church are considerably different than ours?

WHERE THE CHURCH WENT WRONG

SOMEWHERE BEHIND THE PULPIT

The institutional church system has made several fundamental mistakes, which have rendered it irrelevant and impotent. As a result, we have squandered our resources and lost the culture.

The first, unfortunately, is the bedrock characteristic of the modern church: paid, professional pastors. It has caused the paradigm that no one questions: *Every church must be led by a professional pastor.*

It's hard to imagine a church without a paid, professional pastor. In fact, when a congregation faces the lack of one, the acquisition of the missing ingredient becomes the all-important focus of the group. What's the first thing a congregation does when it is faced with its pastor leaving? Put together a team to search for a replacement. Everything is put on hold until the new guy is appointed.

When a congregation begins to grow, what then does it do? It hires more pastors and builds a bigger building.

This characteristic of the American church has so permeated itself into the psyche of the Christian culture and is so deeply embedded into our mindsets that the overwhelming majority of Western Christians have never questioned it. To actually question this bedrock tenant of Western Christianity is to be seen as a wide-eyed radical heretic.

I'm willing to take that risk. If you have come this far with me, you have at least a bit of an open mind. Now, I'm going to ask you to temporarily set aside your preconceived paradigms about this practice and thoughtfully consider the balance of this chapter.

It is my opinion that this tenant of Western Christianity has done more to rob the church of its giftedness, of its power, and of its effectiveness than anything else. That should come as no surprise. After all, Paul observed that when you emphasize "wisdom and eloquence," you "empty the cross of its power."

This practice, and the paradigm which supports it, has diverted our energy and squandered our resources, rendering the church impotent and irrelevant. As a result, we've lost the culture. On a good day, I think of the institutional church system as God's plan B—certainly not what He intended, but He will compromise and work with it. On a bad day, I think of it as Satan's greatest coup.

Let's reason together.

The Problem with the Pastor System

Okay, I know that some of you don't use the word pastor. You may have ministers, preachers, or priests. It doesn't matter what you call them. They are all specially trained men (or women) who are expected to officiate at the worship services, present a message from the pulpit, preside at weddings and funerals, be active in all sorts of church events and programs, visit the sick, and more or less be the professional Christian leader within the congregation. As one of the pastors I have known described it, "To be the hub of the wheel around which everything revolves." Sort of like a king is to a secular group.

So what's wrong with that? Isn't that the way it should be? How could it be any other way? What would we do without a pastor to lead us?

I agree, it looks good. By having a seminary-trained pastor, the congregation is assured of (or so it seems) an educated person to bring thoughtful lessons from the pulpit. That certainly should be edifying for everyone.

And there is someone to watch over the teaching in the church, to make sure that no one strays off the line. And certainly someone has to officiate at weddings and funerals. And church members are too busy to visit the sick and a pastor/preacher/minister/priest has the time to do that. All of those are good things. So what's the problem?

The problem is this. All of these reasons are mankind's good thinking, but they depart from God's simple practices.

Please understand that I have no problem with pastors, the human beings. Most are well-motivated, Godly people who are striving to fulfill what they believe is God's calling. Truly, some of my best friends are pastors.

While some of the most manipulative and deceitful people I have ever encountered were pastors and missionaries, those folks were probably the minority. For the most part, pastors are good people caught in a bad system. It's the system that is the problem, not the individuals.

The paid, located pastor has become the cornerstone of the modern church and the reason why the church is only a fraction of what it could be. If you want to find a reason for the loss of the culture, for the squandering of billions of dollars of money, for the stunting of the spiritual growth and efficacy of millions of Christians, look no further than the pastor system. It is the primary flaw of the church.

The reason we have pastors is historic, not biblical.

> *The reason we have pastors is historic, not biblical.*

When Martin Luther nailed his thesis to the church doors, he focused on changing the doctrine of the church. He neglected, however, to turn the light of scripture onto the structure of the church. So for generations we have been suffering with a structure that was borrowed from the Roman Catholic Church, which borrowed it from pagan practices,[17] not based on God's clear framework expressed in the New Testament.

That is easily understood. Martin Luther was part of the "clergy." It would be an awful lot to expect that he would examine whether or not there ought to be a "clergy" when he was one. That was his livelihood. It is easier to say, "This idea is wrong," than it is to say, "How I've made my living is essentially sinful. My position should be done away with, and I should be out of a job." Very few people have the courage or conviction to say the latter. So they avoid the subject and point everyone's attention elsewhere. When was the last time you heard a sermon on the biblical organization of the church for example?

The title of priest, used by the Roman Catholic Church and a few other close copies, morphed into the Protestant "pastor." The name changed, although the functions remained remarkably the same. While the titles changed as well, from "Father" to "Reverend," the use of titles continued. In other words, the Protestant reformation and every generation of professional Christian since has given lip service to the structure of the church but has avoided a close, biblical look at it.

Here's a table of the typical functions of the Catholic priest and the Protestant "pastor."

	Catholic Priest	Pastor
The primary interpreter of Scripture to the congregation	X	X
Baptizes	X	X
Officiates at weddings	X	X
Speaks at funerals	X	X
Makes hospital visits	X	X
Administers the business of the congregation	X	Generally, with some exceptions
Teaches the saved	X	X
Evangelizes the lost	X	X
Counsels those in crisis	X	X

Clearly, the only difference between the two positions is the title, and the doctrine.

Unfortunately, the modern-day paid pastor is simply not biblical! No matter how hard you look in the New Testament, you cannot find anything like our modern pastors, anywhere.

In the book of Acts, there are twenty-nine places where groups of Christians are either mentioned or implied. In none of these is there anything equivalent to our modern pastors. The church sprang up, grew, and spread throughout the entire known world in about three hundred years without any pastors!

Yes, there were apostles who taught and evangelized. But these special people were imbued with special knowledge and authority that no pastor in our age would dare to claim. Today's pastors cannot trace their lineage back to the apostles. And the involvement of an apostle in a local group of Christians was the exception, not the rule.

The predominant practice was that groups of disciples sprung up on their own. If you look at Paul's journeys closely, you'll observe that generally when he entered a city, the first thing he did was connect with the Christians who were already there. After he left, the Christians were left on their own, with no person having any kind of authority over the small group. The common practice of the apostles was to trust the new believers to the care and safekeeping of the Holy Spirit.

What about elders? Yes, when a group of Christians had grown sufficiently that some in their midst were conforming their character to that of Christ, those thus qualified were occasionally appointed as elders—a confirmation of the service they had already been providing the disciples.

Aren't pastors elders of a sort? A few could develop into elders. But they'd have to meet the very clear qualifications spelled out in Titus and 1 Timothy. Clearly, these qualifications speak to the development of a person's character and have nothing to do with seminaries or education. A few of the differences: elders are always mentioned in the plural, while a paid pastor is a singular figure; elders are raised up from among the people they serve, while paid pastors are imported from outside the congregation; elders are qualified by virtue of their character, paid pastors are ordained based on their education. The position of paid pastor in our modern churches and the biblical role of elder are light-years apart.

> *The position of paid pastor in our modern churches and the biblical role of "elder" are light years apart.*

Clearly, our modern paid pastors are not (with a few exceptions) biblical elders. They are something else. Something we don't see anywhere in the Bible.

Now, I know what you are thinking. "Wait a minute, doesn't the New Testament expressly create the position of pastor?" What about Ephesians 4: the passage that described the "four-fold ministry," or, depending on your view, "the five-fold ministry"? You are, of course, referring to the passage that is often translated like this:

> So Christ himself gave the apostles, the proph-ets, the evangelists, the pastors and teachers, to equip his people for works of service, so that the body of Christ may be built up until we all reach unity in the faith and in the knowledge of the Son of God and become mature, attaining to the whole measure of the fullness of Christ.
>
> (Ephesians 4:11–13)

If we look a little closer, we'll find that there is no way that passage, or any others in the New Testament, authorize the system of paid pastors. Let's look just a little deeper into this issue.

First, the Elders

In the New Testament, there are three Greek words used to refer to the office we call elder. These are listed below with their dictionary definitions. Following each is a list of the New Testament verses in which those words are used.

Presbuteros—those who presided over the assemblies, those who managed public affairs and administered justice.

- Acts 11:30; Acts 15: 2, 4, 6, 22; Acts 20:17
- Acts 21:18, Titus 1:5, 2 John 1
- 1 Peter 5:1–5, Acts 14: 23, Acts 16:4
- 1 Tim 5: 17, 1 Tim 5:19, 3 John 1

Poimen—a man to whose care and control others have committed themselves, the presiding officer, manager, director of any assembly.

- Matt 9:36, Matt 25: 32, Matt 26:31
- Eph. 4:11, John 21:16, Acts 20:28
- 1 Peter 5:2, Mark 6:34, Mark 14: 27
- Luke 2:8, 15, 18, 20; John 10:2, 12; John 10:11–14

Episcopus—a man charged with the duty of seeing that things to be done by others are done rightly.

- Acts 20:28, Heb. 13:17, 1 Pete 5:2
- Phil 1:1, 1 Tim 3:2, Titus 1:7

Let's first look at the translation of the word "poimen" to "pastor" in Ephesians 4. According to J. W. McGarvey, writing in 1865:

> Although this term occurs in the New Testament 18 times, it is in every other instance rendered Shepherd. In seven of those instances, it is used literally for the man who attends to a flock of sheep; in nine it is applied figuratively to Jesus, and only in this one is it applied to a class of office in the church. Now, there is no good reason for a departure in this single instance from a rendering which would otherwise be uniform throughout the New Testament.[18]

In other words, the original Greek work in Ephesians 4 that is commonly translated as "pastor" should not be translated as "pastor" but more accurately as "elder" or "shepherd."

I'm just speculating here, but I wonder if the reason it was translated as "pastor" instead of "shepherd" had to do with the makeup of the people doing the translating. I suspect that they were all "pastors," people associated with training and educating "pastors" or people who made their living at institutions dedicated to training "pastors."

But the New Testament case is even stronger. That these three words (noted above) all refer to one office can be seen by the fact that the words are used interchangeably in the New Testament. While there are several examples of these, two clear examples are Acts 20:17 and 28 and 1 Peter 5:1–5.

> From Miletus, Paul sent to Ephesus for the elders (Presbuteros) of the church…Keep watch over yourselves and all the flock of which the Holy Spirit has made you overseers (Episcopus). Be shepherds (Poimen) of the church of God, which aradigm—the bought with his own blood.
>
> (Acts 20: 17, 28)

> To the elders (Presbuterous) among you…Be shepherds (Poimen) of God's flock that is under your care, serving as overseers (Episcopus).
>
> (1 Peter 5:1 and 2 [19])

There is then only one position, but three terms which highlight different facets of that position. While "elder" is the most popular term today, any of the translations of any of the three words are equally appropriate: shepherd, manager, overseer, pastor, bishop, administrator.

So the "pastor" referred to in Ephesians 4, in modern terminology, should more accurately be translated as elder, and everyone would understand that the passage was describing that position—not a new office in the church, and certainly not the office around which the whole church pivots.

It should be noted that the Bible never uses the word *poimen* (pastor) to refer to a paid staff position. The pastors in the New Testament are always plural and always refer to the men we often call elders. The concept of the "paid professional pastor" as the individual who is responsible for leading the congregation cannot be found in the New Testament.

Imagine that. Our entire institutional church system is based on the mistranslation of one word in the New Testament.

But wait, you say, aren't our modern day paid pastors really just elders in another sense? Actually, no.

This passage of scripture is, if anything, supporting the position of "elder or shepherd." They are referred to in the plural. One would never have one "elder," for example. They rise up from among the people—they aren't trained in a seminary. They gain their position by the working of the Holy Spirit in their lives, and the folks around them come to look to them for guidance by the relationships they have created and the lives they have lived.

So we have a clear description in the New Testament of God's will and direction for his church. Established by the working of the Holy Spirit through evangelists and the evangelical efforts of simple Christians, a number of people become disciples, and a church coalesces. Gradually, through the working of the Holy Spirit, elders emerge and are eventually recognized as the leaders of the congregation. They meet a set of biblical guidelines articulated in Titus and 1 Timothy. The church grows and spins off sister churches. With this format, Christianity penetrated the entire known world in just a few short years.

So, we have a clear description in the New Testament of God's will and direction for His church. Established by the working of the Holy Spirit through evangelists and the evangelical efforts of simple Christians, a number of people become disciples, and a church coalesces. Gradually, through the working of the Holy Spirit, elders emerge and are eventually recognized as the leaders of the congregation. They meet a set of biblical guidelines articulated in Titus and I Timothy. The church grows and spins off sister churches. With this format, Christianity penetrated the entire known world in just a few short years.

We, however, know better. Instead of God's simple plan for the establishment and reproduction of his church, we have substituted our human designs. We have established the individual paid pastor in the place of the plurality of elders. We have substituted a seminary education as a qualification, in the place of the qualities of character clearly described in the New Testament.

> *We, however, know better. Instead of God's simple plan for the establishment and reproduction of His Church, we have substituted our human designs. We have established the individual paid pastor in the place of the plurality of elders. We have substituted a seminary education as a qualification, in the place of the qualities of character clearly described in the New Testament.*

While the decision seemed good at the time (we can't have a real church without a pastor, can we?), the consequences are here and are bigger than anyone anticipated. We have taken the power of the Holy Spirit out of the church almost completely, substituted our human design, and so we have spent $530 billion, not grown a bit, driven our children away, condoned mediocrity, and lost the culture and inoculate millions from a commitment to Christ.

The apostle's example and clear teaching in the New Testament indicate that the church should be led by elders who are shaped by the Holy Spirit and raise up out of the people in the church.

The institutional church system says that a congregation should be led by a seminary-trained professional pastor.

If that paradigm—the concept that every congregation must be led by a professional pastor—is erroneous, what else could we believe about the church that may also be nonbiblical?

Could it be that the institutional church system isn't the church of the New Testament?

> *If that paradigm—the concept that every congregation must be led by a professional pastor— is erroneous, what else could we believe about the church that may also be non-biblical? Could it be that the institutional church system isn't the church of the New Testament?*

Thinking About This Chapter

Have you ever wondered why we expect every church to be led by a professional pastor?

Has it ever occurred to you that "pastors," in the modern sense of the word, are nowhere found in the New Testament?

To what extent does your congregation have biblical elders?

Has it ever occurred to you that where we have biblical elders, there is no need for a pastor, and where we have pastors, there are rarely biblical elders?

If the practice of professional, paid pastors as leaders of a congregation is unbiblical, what other practices could we be following that are likewise unbiblical?

BEYOND THE BIBLICAL CASE—PRACTICAL IMPLICATIONS

IT'S NOT JUST SCRIPTURE

That should be enough to convict us of the poison of the paid pastor system. But a thinking person with an open, inquisitive mind will soon uncover a number of other issues which lead us to the point where we have to say, "What were we thinking when we hired a pastor? How did we go so wrong?" Let's examine a number of them.

1. The Natural Inclination of the Paid Pastor Has Led to a Christianity So Divided and Fractured That It Defies Explanation.

Let's start with Jesus's last recorded prayer, in John 17:20–23:

> My prayer is not for them alone. I pray also
> for those who will believe in me through their

> message, that all of them may be one, Father, just as you are in me and I am in you. May they also be in us so that the world may believe that you have sent me. I have given them the glory that you gave me, that they may be one as we are one—I in them and you in me—so that they may be brought to complete unity. Then the world will know that you sent me and have loved them even as you have loved me.

He passionately prays for unity among his people, acknowledging that unity among Christians is a sign to the world that we are of Christ. By implication, a lack of unity indicates the opposite. Yet our man-made system of paid, professional pastors fosters division.

Christianity continues to splinter into smaller and smaller segments, called denominations. The man-made leaders find reasons to separate themselves from other groups, rallying their followers around some issue that is expounded by the educated leaders but generally of little initial concern of the people and build institutions based on a man-made distinction.

The result? Thousands of denominations and a skepticism (rightly so) on the part of the non-Christian world.

Thousands of denominations and a skepticism (rightly so) on the part of the non-Christian world.

Is the Institutional Church
Really the Church?

A few years ago, at a time in which I was heavily involved in my local church, the congregation went through a nasty split. It shocked me. I've since learned, however, that congregational divisions are something that happens regularly. See if any of this sounds familiar.

Here's what happened. There arose some differences of opinion between the elders and the senior pastor regarding to authority in the church. The pastor had been in the congregation for eleven years and had grown more and more comfortable with his self-defined role as the "hub of the wheel," the center of all activity, connected to every ministry or effort in the church. Although never appointed as such, and not qualified, he began to refer to himself as the chief elder.

His position grew steadily more hardened, and eventually, he announced, unexpectedly, on a Thursday evening that, "We're going to have a family event. It can be either the birth of a new church or a nasty divorce." The choice was ours (the elders). The following Sunday, three days later, he was gone, along with about one-third of the congregation. He had been manipulating behind the scenes to pull off this dramatic split.

At that time, I felt like I had been blindsided. I had no idea things like this actually happened in Christian churches. The pastor's deceit and manipulation was a complete shock to me. To say I was disillusioned would be putting it mildly.

Since then, I've learned that this was hardly an isolated event. Within a few weeks of the event, I discovered an acquaintance who had lived through an almost identical situation in his Presbyterian church. Next I learned of a large independent congregation not far from us who had gone through an amazingly similar situation a few years earlier.

As I became more aware of church splits, I found more and more examples of them throughout the Christian world. At about the same time, one of the largest churches in our area, a two thousand plus congregation, lived through almost exactly the same experience. In the Sunday newspaper, there appeared a large add by the pastor, accompanied, of course, by his picture, advertising his new congregation and attempting to lure people to follow after him.

As I investigated this phenomenon, I discovered that this is hardly new. In fact, most of the thousands of Christian denominations in this country have their beginnings in a pastor splitting from his former congregation or affiliation.

The local newspaper contained a story about a denomination headquartered in my hometown, which was going through the pain of a split. Prominent in the newspaper was the name and comments of the pastor who seemed to be the galvanizing focus for the disaffected.

This can hardly be pleasing to a Lord who prays for unity. But yet it continues.

Why is that?

The most visible job of the paid pastor is to preach the sermon, right? So that means he spends much of his time arranging scripture passages to support the points he wants to make.

It is in the nature of teachers, particularly teachers of adults, to want to get the subject right. They obsess about this word or that word, this phrase or that one. Trust me, I know that because I am one. I was educated as a teacher and have spent much of my adult life teaching salespeople, sales managers, and sales executives.

Not only do they obsess with getting the words right, their antennas are fine-tuned to anyone else who doesn't. My wife recently commented about one of our acquaintances, "You can tell she is a retired teacher because she is always correcting people." It's ingrained in the personality.

The net impact of this is the natural tendency to emphasize doctrine and to find fault with the other guy's views. Being right becomes of uttermost importance. If you're right, then the other guy must be wrong, if he doesn't agree 100 percent with you.

And that, alas, is the primary reason why we have forty thousand different denominations in this country, countless thousands of church splits, and millions of disaffected Christians.[19] In almost every case, it was an instance of a professional pastor disagreeing with someone and deciding to lead his flock to a more pure doctrinal position. At the heart of almost every split, and the beginning of every denomination, is a professional pastor leading a group away.

Stop for a minute, and imagine you are that alien from another planet, sent to make observations about earth's customs and culture. You come across Christianity and are impressed with Jesus's final prayer:

"That they all might be one, just as I am one in you" (John 17:21).

Then, you see that same movement fractured into forty thousand different subgroups and many of the congregations splitting even further. You would have to conclude that those folks, the ones who split themselves into all these differing groups, could not possibly be the same as those who follow the Christ. If unity is the sign to the world that we are Christians, is a lack of unity a sign that we are not?

> *If unity is a sign to the world that we are Christians, is lack of unity a sign that we are not?*

If we are really Christians, how could we have, generation after generation, done exactly the opposite for what He prayed?

Something is terribly wrong here.

Now, put yourself in the place of the average non-Christian, who sees the same thing. This can't be Christianity he or she thinks. There is something terribly wrong here.

And of course he would be right. It's the professional pastor system.

2. The Professional Pastor System Has Siphoned the Resources Away from the Work of the Church

A congregation not far from my home recently announced a special fund drive. They needed $600,000 to upgrade the audio and video system in the sanctuary. Let me repeat that, to make sure you got it: They needed $600,000 to upgrade the audio and video system in the sanctuary.

Have you ever been to a developing country? Do you have any idea of what $600,000 could do? Do you know how many microbusinesses could be created, how many jobs created, how many clean water systems developed? Do you know how many widows and orphans could be supported by $600,000?

Let's put this in perspective:

> Religion that God our Father accepts as pure and faultless is this: to look after orphans and widows in their distress and to keep oneself from being polluted by the world.
>
> (James 1:27)

So on one hand, we have the clear New Testament direction to look after orphans and widows, and on the other, we have the decision to spend $600,000 on new AV equipment.

I was visiting the day the senior pastor announced the fund drive. He made a compelling case for it. That's what happens. When we get inside of an institution, an organization, or a system, we naturally see the world from that entity's perspective. It's not just the institutional church, it's every institution. It's why government bureaucracies always grow and always need more money, it's why college tuition always goes up, it's why public school teachers always need more funds. It's why the manufacturers of buggy whips thought the solution was to increase the quality of their product when the gasoline-powered engine was rendering horse drawn carriages obsolete. It's why politicians who have never worked in private enterprise see the government as the answer to all problems. When you are inside an entity, you just naturally see needs and opportunities inside that entity. Your viewpoint becomes narrow, your focus generated by the insider's perspective.

So a group of pastors who run a congregation naturally see a continuous stream of needs for more resources devoted to that institution. They have this big building, a large number of people attending Sunday morning services, and an electronic system growing old. From that perspective, it makes perfect sense.

Again, it's not the people. Pastors are generally good people, well-motivated, trying to do what they think the Lord wants them to do. But they are hindered by a flawed system and a set of debilitating paradigms.

It takes someone from the outside, looking in, to see the contradiction. How can we claim to be Christ's church, when we spend the vast majority of our money on ourselves?

> *How can we claim to be Christ's church, when we*
> *spend the vast majority of our money on ourselves?*

Now add that very rational $600,000 request to all the other needs of the institution. A new classroom, a new air-conditioner, new carpeting, a new building, a new associate pastor, a pastor for spiritual formation, another one for worship arts, another one for this, and another one for that. Add it all up, and it is 530 billion dollars; we haven't grown a bit, and we've lost the culture.

In the big picture, we have siphoned billions and billions of dollars from the work of the Lord and spent it on our institutions, on buildings and pastors and denominations, and headquarters and conferences and newsletters and the list goes on and on. How could we have let this happen?

> *Forgive me, Father, for being a part of this system*
> *which has squandered your resources so blatantly,*
> *that has neglected your work for our self-centered*
> *interpretation of our own. How could I have been*
> *a part of this for so long? Father, I am really,*
> *really sorry.*

3. The Professional Pastor System Has
   Led to a Dumbing-Down of People's
   Spiritual Intelligence and Maturity.

I know what you are thinking. Wait a minute, the
primary purpose of the "four-fold ministry" (or five-
fold, depending on your interpretation) is to build up
the church, to bring people to maturity. Isn't that what
it says?

Yep. It says

> So Christ himself gave the apostles, the proph-
> ets, the evangelists, the pastors and teachers, to
> equip his people for works of service, so that
> the body of Christ may be built up until we all
> reach unity in the faith and in the knowledge of
> the Son of God and become mature, attaining
> to the whole measure of the fullness of Christ.
>
> (Ephesians 4:11–13)

Unfortunately, it is the very rare congregation that
actually does this. It's not hard to understand. If we
have substituted our human institutions in the place
of God's divine organization, why wouldn't we expect
the results, as well, to be something other than what
He intended?

If we had really equipped people for works of service,
why would we have so few people actually doing any?
The vast majority of churchgoers see Christianity as

being defined by attending church on Sunday morning and then going about your business as if it didn't exist.

Works of service, from the inside of the institution, mean things that the institution wants done, that further ingrain it into the conscience of the congregation. So we can have a little training on "being a deacon" or "financial stewardship." Our works of service are defined by things like taking up the collection, passing out communion, singing and playing an instrument, teaching a children's class, or making coffee for the congregation. Notice that all of these things address the needs of the institution, not the needs of the lost world around us.

I spend the vast majority of my time in the marketplace, interacting with salespeople and business owners. In my entire lifetime, I have never had a church-sponsored training session on how to do that in more godly way. I've never heard a sermon address it.

One of my friends, a mature, seasoned CEO of a growing multimillion dollar company, once remarked that it's only in church that his gifts, experience, wisdom, and insight are not seen as valuable. "If I'm good," he said to me, "in a couple of years they may ask me to help take up the collection."

Unfortunately the professional pastor system means that strong, mature, gifted Christian men and women are more likely seen as threats than as assets. You're welcome to be a part of the congregation, as long as you sit in the pews, listen to the pastor, and don't raise any hard questions.

> *Unfortunately the professional pastor system means that strong, mature, gifted Christian men and women are more likely seen as threats than as assets. You're welcome to be a part of the congregation, as long as you sit in the pews, listen to the pastor, and don't raise any hard questions.*

I had a personal experience that illustrates this point. At one point, I was teaching the adult Sunday school class in the congregation we attended. The congregation went through the process of replacing the pastor. When the new man was hired, the very first thing he did was remove me from the position and take over himself. I remember the moment to this day. It was just before the worship service was to begin. He came up, introduced himself, and thanked me for taking care of the class. He would take over next Sunday, he announced.

The message was clear. The A team had arrived, and it was time for the B team to step aside. Let me put this in perspective. I have both a bachelor of education and a master of arts in teaching degrees. I taught for four years after graduation, was rated a master teacher, and have spent the last twenty-five years teaching salespeople, sales managers and sales executives. In other words, when it comes to teaching, I'm no slouch.

But it didn't matter. It didn't matter what gifts I had nor what education or experience. The professional had arrived and the second-class Christians could resume their place in the pews.

I know that mind-set is common and that there are millions of other gifted Christians who have been shunted aside in order to allow the professionals to shine.

When you think of the typical church service, what do you think of? Some singing and a sermon. The pastor talks, and anywhere from a couple of dozen to several thousand people listen. One person is active, and the rest passive. Passively listening becomes the behavior that is expected. Can you imagine what would happen if you stood up in the middle of a sermon and said, "Excuse me, I have a question." Unthinkable.

That passivity which is encouraged in the worship service just naturally spills over to every other aspect of church life.

4. The Professional Pastor System Has Caused Millions of Christians to Think of Themselves As Second Class, Robbing Them of Their Giftedness and God's Purpose for Their Lives.

For much of my adult life, I saw myself as a "second-class Christian," defined by a very familiar paradigm. See if it doesn't sound familiar.

> Real ministry is defined by the time you spend in the official efforts of the church to evangelize the lost and edify the saved. This is the work that God is interested in, that He considers most important, special and significant.

If you are like most Christians, you are nodding your head, thinking, "Of course, who would ever question that?"

The expressions of this are all around us. Remember, paradigms shape our attitudes and determine our behavior. So we can look at attitudes and behavior and use them to discover the paradigm which lies under the surface.

Here are some examples of this paradigm in practice. One of my clients recently indicated to me that one of his salespeople had left the company to go into the full-time ministry. We all know what he means by that. This person is going to make his living in some sanctioned work of some church. That's real ministry. What he was doing before was just making a living. Or so we have been conditioned to think.

A few years ago, I read Bob Buford's book entitled *Halftime*. I was impressed with it and bought several to give to friends. The premise of the book, written primarily to Christian business people, was now that in the first half of your life you have achieved some degree of success, use the second half to do something significant. Donate your time, money, and talents to a ministry. Your work was just work and not significant, another expression of the paradigm.

It's not unusual to hear a pastor or fellow Christian talking about God's work or referring to the church building as God's house. This kind of language indicates, of course, that God is more interested in these things than He is other things, which are not God's work or places which are not God's house.

I could cite hundreds of other examples, but you get the idea. This concept of ministry is a deeply held, pervasive paradigm, which is embraced to some degree by almost all of twenty-first century Christendom.

But let's take a moment to consider the implications of this paradigm. Consider that if some work is significant, what does that say about other work? Insignificant.

If some effort is special, what does that say about other work? Ordinary.

If some work is important, what does that say about other work? Unimportant.

> *Consider that if some work is significant,*
> *what does that say about other work?*
> *Insignificant.*
> *If some effort is special, what does*
> *that say about other work?*
> *Ordinary.*
> *If some work is important, what does*
> *that say about other work?*
> *Unimportant.*

In other words, if we hold church work to be special, significant and important, then this says the rest of our lives are ordinary, insignificant and unimportant. So we really are second class Christians!

But is that what the Bible teaches? Hardly. In fact, it's just the opposite. For example, Paul said that everything we do, if we do it as a service to Christ, is important:

> Whatever you do, work at it with all your heart,
> as working for the Lord, not for human mas-
> ters, since you know that you will receive an
> inheritance from the Lord as a reward. It is the
> Lord Christ you are serving.
>
> (Colossians 3:23–24)

A few years ago, I became interested in the definition of "minister." Since ministry is clearly important
to the ICS, there must be a definition in the Bible for
who a minister is and what work constitutes ministry. I searched for months until I came to a conclusion: Clearly "ministry" in the Bible is not determined
by what is done but rather by for whom it is done.
Whatever you do for Christ is ministry.

---

*Clearly ministry in the Bible is not determined
by what is done, but rather by for whom it is
done. Whatever you do for Christ is ministry.*

God's work and will for this world is far greater
than just those activities we know as church work. God
desires to extend the kingdom into every aspect of his
creation. And He expects us to be obedient to him and
offer our lives as ministry to extend his influence into
every nook and cranny of his world. When we go to a
meeting at our children's school, we are taking Christ's
influence with us, extending his impact into that aspect
of creation. When we go to work, we are extending

Christ's influence into those contacts with people with whom we connect. When we talk with a neighbor, fill the car up with gas, cut the grass, or shop for groceries, we are Christ's ambassadors, extending his influence into those realms.

Jesus called us to be the salt of the world. He intentionally chose that analogy. Salt has no value when it is held inside the salt shaker crushed against other grains of salt. It is only when it is mixed with other things that salt imparts its influence on that around it. So too for us. When we are huddled with one another in the confines of church buildings, we are not fulfilling the ministry that God appointed to us. While time together is necessary for encouragement and equipping, it's a means to an end. The end is our influence in the ministries that we call our lives.

If "every congregation must be led by a professional pastor" is a false paradigm, what else do we believe about church that may be wrong? Could it be that the institutional church system is not really the church?

If "Every congregation must be led by a professional pastor" is a false paradigm, what else do we believe about 'church' that may be wrong? Could it be that the institutional church system is not really the church?

Thinking About This Chapter

How do you explain, and accept, the division which is the characteristic of modern Western Christianity, in light of Jesus's prayer for unity?

If unity is a sign that we are Christians, is the lack of unity a sign that we are not?

How do you justify $530 billion spent on ourselves and no increase in the percentage of Christians in this country?

To what degree can you relate to the CEO who said, "If I'm good, in a couple of years, they may ask me to help take up the collection"?

To what extent have you observed strong, mature, and gifted Christians who are shunted to the sidelines in your congregation?

If the efforts of your local congregation are God's work or holy or special, what does that say about your life?

To what degree does your church teach that ministry has nothing to do with roles in the church?

BUT THAT'S NOT ALL

Alas, the mistake of creating a system based on human notions of what is good and right and proper—the professional pastor system—has just naturally lead to some other mistakes that have compounded and multiplied the negative consequences. In the next two chapters, I explore a number of those.

WORSHIP SERVICES

If there is any paradigm more deeply embedded in the psyche of the Western Christian, I don't know what it would be. The paradigm is this: *Going to church means attending the Sunday morning worship service. It is the heart of Christianity.* It has become the point of convergence for the average Christian. It's what we think of when we think of going to church. When we invite someone to church, that means we invite them to a worship service. It is the ultimate expression of the local congregation, the experience that causes some to go and some to stay, the shining focal point of the preacher's skills.

While it may be possible to conceive of a church without a pastor, at least for a temporary period, it is impossible to imagine a church without a worship service. That is what church is all about, isn't it? Isn't it what defines a church? In other words, if you don't have a worship service, you're really not a church. Nothing is more central to Western Christians.

What if worship services were not in the Bible?

They aren't. You cannot find a single instance of a worship service anywhere in the New Testament. The word does not appear in the Bible. In fact, the Bible's plain teaching would never lead you to create what happens in our church buildings every Sunday.

Let's unpack this. This passage in Romans precisely defines worship for us.

> Therefore, I urge you, brothers and sisters, in view of God's mercy, to offer your bodies as a living sacrifice, holy and pleasing to God—this is your true and proper worship.
>
> (Romans 12:1)

Worship, according to the New Testament, is about living your life in such a way as to give of yourself to God and others. It is a far deeper and more intimate thing—a way of life, really.

Ah, but since we know better, we have chosen to redefine it in human terms. Biblical worship is far too demanding for us. So we've created a false paradigm to ease our conscience and make it easier. Just show up once a week, sing a few songs, and listen to the pastor talk for a half hour and you've been a Christian this week.

I know, sometimes the songs are inspiring. And sometimes the message is moving. And we've got to have a collection. And in some churches, at some times, we'll have what we call the Lord's Supper. It feels good. It makes us feel good to know that we've done our duty, taken the kids to children's church, and said hello to four people sitting around us whom we don't know very well, if at all.

And because we have substituted a man-made construction for God's plan, our children are leaving in droves, we're turning off millions of Christ-seekers, we condone mediocrity, we've spent 530 billion dollars, we've lost the culture, and we are inoculating most of the population from committing to Christ.

Something is wrong.

This is one of the major things.

But you are saying, what about 1 Corinthians 14 and Paul's teaching about worship? Let's take a look.

> What then shall we say, brothers? When you come together, each of you has a hymn, or a word of instruction, a revelation, a tongue or an interpretation. All of these must be done for the strengthening of the church. If anyone speaks in a tongue, two—or at the most three—should speak, one at a time, and someone must interpret. If there is no interpreter, the speaker should keep quiet in the church and speak to himself and to God.

> Two or three prophets should speak, and the others should weigh carefully what is said. And if a revelation comes to someone who is sitting down, the first speaker should stop. For you can all prophesy in turn so that everyone may be instructed and encouraged. The spirits of proph-

ets are subject to the control of prophets. For God is not a God of disorder but of peace...

But if anyone ignores this, they will themselves be ignored.

Therefore, my brothers, be eager to prophesy, and do not forbid speaking in tongues. But everything should be done in a fitting and orderly way.

(1 Corinthians 14:26–40)

In this passage, Paul describes the meeting of the church and gives some guidelines. Notice, first of all that it is a church meeting, not a worship service. Worship is clearly not the purpose. He tells us what the purpose of the church meeting is: *Everything must be done for the strengthening of the church.*

So the meeting is about building up the church. Interesting, the same function as the "five-fold ministry" in Ephesians. To turn this meeting into a worship service is to twist God's intentions. It feels good to us, but it's clearly not what He intended.

Notice the way Christians are to go about meeting together in order to build each other up. They are to sing four songs performed by people on a stage and listen to the pastor lecture for a half hour. Actually, it does *not* say that. It says something quite a bit different. The folks at the meeting should actively participate in building one another up. Paul has to give them some rules, because it sounds like the meetings were so full of participation that they were getting a bit rowdy.

Here's what he said: "Each of you has a hymn, or a word of instruction, a revelation, a tongue or an interpretation" (1 Corinthians 14:26).

He could have said, "One of you should preach to the rest, and they should sit passively until he is done." But he didn't. He said, "Each of you." Now, it takes a seminary-trained pastor to read that and think "each of you" means "just one of you." Each one is to participate and bring something edifying to share. Everyone is expected to participate. Christianity is not a spectator sport. It's an active lifestyle.

Let's pretend you are that alien from another planet, sent to earth to make observations about the habits of earthlings. You've researched a bit and discovered this passage of 1 Corinthians. "Okay," you think, "I'll spot these Christians by the way they meet together." And off you go, in search of Christian meetings. You stroll by sporting events, concerts, and the occasional political rally. "Not there," you think. You pop your head in a couple of churches and think, "Another concert," and move on. You think it a little odd that these entertainment events occur on Sunday mornings instead of Friday nights, as it seems most do, but that's not a big deal. People seem to be having a much better time at the concerts and football games. But you press on, continuing to look for those small group, interactive, building-each-other-up meetings.

If you were an objective alien, you would never guess that the Sunday morning worship service had any relation at all to the description Paul gave.

"But," you are thinking to yourself, "it's traditional. I can't imagine being a Christian without going to a worship service."

I understand. That's exactly the problem. We've bought a man-made paradigm that is so deeply embedded in our psyche that we can't imagine it being gone.

Of course, Jesus did say...

> Jesus answered, "Isaiah was right when he spoke about you hypocrites. He wrote: These people show honor to me with words, but their hearts are far from me. Their worship of me is worthless. The things they teach are nothing but human rules.
>
> (Isaiah 29:13)

> You have stopped following the commands of God, and you follow only human teachings. Then Jesus said to them, "You cleverly ignore the commands of God so you can follow your own teachings."
>
> (Mark 7:6–9 New Century Version)

Could worship services be a specific, tangible expression of this truth? Are we teaching the worship service as doctrine? Not only that, are we supporting it with guilt trips issued from the pulpit and referring to it as "church"? Is our practice of defining church as "worship service" so far away from God's clear directions to us that we have spent 530 billion dollars, not grown a bit and lost the culture?

Something is very, very wrong. And this is part of it. Let's start adding this up.

On one hand, we have the clear teaching of the New Testament, and on the other, we have the common practices and supporting paradigms of the institutional church system.

Church of the New Testament	Institutional Church System
Lead by a plurality of elders, who are shaped by the Holy Spirit and arise out of the local church.	Lead by a paid professional pastor, who was educated at a seminary.
Meet together in an interactive, participatory meeting.	Sing three songs and listen to one person speak in very large groups.
Father, I repent of my agreement with this human construct of worship services. I will worship you as you indicated, with my whole life. Forgive me, Father, for buying into this paradigm and promoting it to my family and friends. I'm so very sorry for the part I had in accepting this and losing the culture.	

Church Buildings

Here's the argument. If we don't have church buildings, where can we have our worship services? It is supported by the paradigm: "Every church must have its own church building."

Are you beginning to see a pattern here? If we have paid pastors, they need to have some place to preach to the congregation because that's what they have been trained to do. So we better gather the congregation together so they can be preached to all at once, or maybe in two or three separate gatherings.

Since we need to have them all together in a big group, let's create these things we call a worship service and sell it to the people as "church," making them feel guilty if they don't attend. Now, since we have these worship services, we better have a building. Never mind that we use it for just a few hours a week. Never mind that the money spent on church buildings in the United States is probably enough to lift 50 percent of the world's poor out of poverty. We need to have a building.

Since we have a pastor and a worship service, we must have a building. And alas, those two things become the focal point of our finances and of our resources. We can't really give much to missions, because we have to pay for the building and support the pastor.

Stop for a minute, and consider this. How much good could that money, which is given for the church building and the pastor, how much could it do, if we didn't have to support a pastor and pay for a building?

And so we have spent 530 billion dollars, not grown a bit and lost the culture.

You know, of course, there is no biblical mandate to have a church building. You can't find one anywhere in the New Testament. It is purely a man-made idea, designed to provide a large place where a pastor can preach to a large group of people. Since preaching is what pastors do, they need a place to do it. Ergo, church buildings.

It is my belief that, if you read the New Testament objectively, you'd gain the impression that church is primarily a small group relationship. The New

Testament is replete with "one another" commands. The larger the group, the more difficult it is to "one another" each other.

Jim Rutz, in his landmark book *The Open Church*,[20] written twenty years ago, attributed the establishment of church buildings by Constantine in AD 300 as the single event that changed the course of the church and robbed it of its power.

George Barna and Frank Viola, writing in *Pagan Christianity*,[21] provided a detailed description of how church buildings evolved from pagan practices.

The church building and the inevitable additions, renovations, and maintenance suck the resources out of the church and provide an atmosphere that is antithesis to simple New Testament Christianity.

Church of the New Testament	Institutional Church System
Lead by a plurality of elders, who are shaped by the Holy Spirit, and arise out of the local church.	Lead by a paid professional pastor, who was educated at a seminary.
Met together in an interactive, participatory meeting.	Sing three songs and listen to one person speak in very large groups.
Met in people's homes.	Meet in church buildings.

Father, forgive me for attending worship services in church buildings. I meant well; I was just misled. Forgive me for the part I had in supporting these man-made efforts, and this human institution. I'm sorry, Lord.

Thinking About This Chapter

Have you ever wondered why we have worship services when there is no biblical example of them or mandate for them?

To what extent have you been taught about biblical worship? Romans 12:1

How do you justify worship services with Paul's specific directions for church meetings in 1 Corinthians 14?

Is it possible that church should not have buildings?

What would happen to your church if it had to give up its building?

Would that be a bad thing or a good thing?

A COUPLE MORE THINGS

THIS CONGREGATION MUST GROW

O f course! Who could question that?

This is another one of those paradigms that support and empower the institutional church system, and that exist completely outside of the New Testament directives. Specifically, the paradigm commands, "This congregation must grow!"

If you're involved in a congregation, I'm sure that the subject of congregational growth has come up over and over again. It's given as the reason for a whole host of pulpit-directed efforts.

We have to raise money for a building fund. Why? Because the congregation needs to grow.

We need to hire a youth minister. Why? Because the congregation has to grow.

We need to create these new programs. Why? Because the congregation has to grow.

And so on and so forth. Now, have you ever seen anyone question the assumption that "the congregation must grow"? Anybody stand up in a congregational meeting and say, "Why?" Any brave soul write a letter to the editor (usually the pastor/preacher/minister/priest) of the newsletter asking the question why?

Probably not. That's one of the unquestioned beliefs that no one dares question. To do so would subject you to the whispered judgment of a majority of the people. It's just not done. Culturally unacceptable. Unchristian.

Too bad. It ought to be questioned.

Before we consider the biblical view, let's analyze the practical consequences of congregation growth. What happens when congregations make major efforts to grow?

First, the process of growth is often expensive, requiring funding to build new buildings, put on new programs, hire new staff, pay for advertising, newsletters, et cetera. While all of this seems good, the reality is that it often moves the focus of the church from the simple message of the Gospel to the more complex message promoting "our church." Congregational members become involved in church programs, church messages, and church initiatives, which substitute the "church" for the Gospel.

Then, there are the effects of successful church growth programs. On the one hand, the worship service has more people and seems more exciting and uplifting. There often are more hands available for church programs, so the core group doesn't need to volunteer for everything. They get a little break. Since the congregation is now larger, the weekly collection is bigger. That means that you can hire additional professional staff to take over what church members were doing before. No need to have a volunteer organize a youth ministry; you can now afford a professional. No need to have a member of the congregation teach a Sunday school class; you have an associate pastor who can do that. As the congregation grows, it can afford more professional staff, maybe a full-time church secretary, hey, maybe even a pastor of administration!

All of this seems good. You can invite your friends to Sunday worship knowing that you won't be embarrassed by amateur performances. Seems good.

But there is a devastating flip side. As the congregation grows, often more and more of the budget is siphoned off to the support of professionals, the funding of programs, and the building of buildings. The more money and energy devoted to these things, the less devoted to the simple work of the church. The more clerks, bureaucrats, and professionals your church employs, the less need for involvement on the part of the people. God's charge that we are all ministers and priests becomes just a hollow statement that is ignored or given lip service but not really pursued. The more professional and polished is your worship service, the more it encourages spectator Christianity. Often, the net result of congregational growth is the super involvement of a few and the alienation and marginalization of the vast majority.

You and your family could be one of them. As the congregation grows, often it only succeeds in building a larger bureaucracy and a bigger building, leaving the vast majority of members in spiritual sleep.

That's the devastating consequence of congregational growth. You and your family could very well be sucked into the effort, causing you to change your focus from the simple Gospel of Christ to the building fund, the search for another professional, or the management of another pulpit-directed program.

Or you could be left on the margins, expected to be a spectator in the growing professionalization of the congregation. No longer necessary—thanks for your time, now move over and let the professionals do it.

What seems good to mankind is actually devastating to much of the congregation. Man's "good" substitutes for God's best.

But what about the biblical view? Isn't it mandated that congregations grow?

No!

The great commission given to the church in Matthew 28:19 says:

> Therefore go and make disciples of all nations, baptizing them in the name of the Father and of the Son and of the Holy Spirit, and teaching them to obey everything I have commanded you. And surely I will be with you always, to the very end of the age.

Jesus did not say, "Stay, therefore, around your neighborhood, inviting people to church, building ever-bigger buildings and programs."

Okay, I know that not everyone can be a foreign missionary, etcetera. However, the point is that Jesus said, "Make disciples, baptize, and teach." He did not say, "Build the local congregation."

The mistake we make is when we believe that building the local congregation is a means to the end of evangelizing the world. The truth is that it is generally a substitute for it! Normally, when we're building the local church, we're engaged in activities that substitute for pure Christianity. We invite our saved neighbors to church; we don't invite our unsaved friends to Christ. We encourage our kids to support the youth ministry instead of teaching them at home.

What would happen to Christianity in this country if we believed that it is Christ's church that must grow, not necessarily our local congregation? What would happen if we focused on Christ, not church? Wouldn't we be more active in promoting Christ, not our church? When someone came to Christ, wouldn't we be more concerned about personally discipling him/her instead of seeing to it that they got shuffled to the appropriate class? If our congregation did grow, what would happen if instead of building a new building and hiring new staff, we encouraged a group to form their own small church? Wouldn't the net result be more people active, more leaders created, more personal ministry, less money spent on bricks and a mortgage, less money spent on professional clergy, and Christ's church growing more rapidly?

The paradigm that our congregation must grow is one of the most deceptive of them all. It seems like such a good idea. But remember, mankind's good is a poor substitute for God's best.

What's the impact on you and your family? Energy, money, gifts, and talents wasted. Instead of building a relationship with Christ, you're in danger of focusing on the efforts of the church. Relationships, no; programs, *yes*. The further away you and your family move from the purity of Christianity, the sadder and more unfulfilled are your lives. Focus your energy and your family's on the "congregation must grow," and you are likely to look back in sadness and regret a number of years from now.

BAPTISM

I just don't know why some of this is so difficult. Are we so gullible that we can't discern the simple plain teaching of the Bible? Evidently we are.

This paradigm, in the historic sense, is a relatively new development: "To become a Christian, just ask Jesus into your heart."

Here's a verse with which we are all familiar. Please forgive my paraphrase: It's Jesus's final charge to his disciples:

> All power in heaven and on earth is given to me. So go and make disciples of all people in the world, teaching them to ask me into their hearts. Teach them to obey everything that I have taught you, and I will be with you always, even until the end of this age.
>
> (Matthew 28:18–20 [paraphrased])

What's wrong with that verse? Even the most imma-ture Christian will recognize the problem immediately. Jesus didn't say, "Ask Jesus into their hearts." You say, Jesus said, "Baptizing them in the name of the Father and the Son and the Holy Spirit." (Matthew 28:18)

That's right. How could I have gotten that wrong? And here I thought that when He said "baptizing" He really meant "ask me into their hearts." Could it be that when He said "baptizing" He meant "baptizing"?

The biblical case for baptism is overwhelming.

1. Jesus was baptized before He began His ministry. Note that He did not attempt any ministry until He had been baptized. By the way, what happened immediately following Jesus's baptism, as He was coming up out of the water?

> At that moment, heaven was opened, and He saw the Spirit of God descending like a dove and lighting on him. And a voice from heaven said, "This is my Son, whom I love; with him I am well pleased."
>
> (Mathew 3:16–17)

I wonder if there was any connection between his baptism at the beginning of his ministry, the appearance of the Holy Spirit and the Father's pro-nouncement. At this point, what had He done in his ministry? Not a thing except to be baptized.

2. Jesus commanded the disciples to baptize every dis-ciple. See Mathew 28 discussed above.

3. Peter, in the first speech following Pentecost, when the Jewish audience was convicted of their sin, asking, "What shall we do?" said, "Say a prayer, asking Jesus into your heart."

   Actually, that's not what he said. What he did say was, "Repent and be baptized, every one of you, in the name of Jesus Christ so that your sins may be forgiven. And you will receive the gift of the Holy Spirit" (Acts 2:38).
   Peter was just being obedient, doing what Jesus did, and what he commanded Peter to do.

4. In every instance of someone coming to Christ in the rest of the New Testament, they are always immediately baptized. No exceptions. Every single time. Check it out:

   • Acts 2:41–That's the story of three thousand being baptized at Pentecost. Imagine that. It's the middle of the morning, in Jerusalem, how easy would it have been to arrange to baptize, spur of the moment, three thousand people? If it were okay to just ask Jesus into their hearts, wouldn't Peter have told them to do that?
   • Acts 8:12–Samaritans are converted and baptized.
   • Acts 8: 36–The story of the Ethiopian eunuch, who is baptized, in the desert, in the very first available place, at the earliest possible time. Think of that: In the middle of the desert. Why didn't Stephen just tell him to ask Jesus into his

heart? Was it really necessary that they stop everything and baptize him? Evidently it was.

- Acts 9: 18–Saul (Paul), the first thing he had to do when he was able, before anything else, was to be baptized.
- Acts 10: 47–Cornelius and his entire household are baptized the day of their conversion.
- Acts 16:15–Lydia and all her household are baptized the instant of their conversion.

Once again, the objective, nonchurch raised person, the person who did not attend a seminary, would read that overwhelming case and conclude that if he wanted to follow Christ, he better be baptized, and he better do it as soon as possible.

Very few of our churches teach that truth, however. I understand that it is inconvenient to baptize people when you've got a thousand of them in a big auditorium and the next worship service starts in twenty minutes. It really is much more convenient just to tell them to stand at their seat and say a prayer, and a couple of months from now, we'll see about having a baptism service.

I don't know how God will deal with the hundreds of thousands of pastors who tell people to say a prayer instead of being baptized upon their conversion to Christ. Nor do I know how He will deal with the millions of believers who have not been taught about this simple act of submission, which is the rite of initiation into the Christian faith.

All I know is that God said His ways are different than our ways and that obedience is better than sacrifice.

I am called, as is every other Christian, to be obedient.

Church of the New Testament	Institutional Church System
Lead by a plurality of elders, who are shaped by the Holy Spirit, and arise out of the local church.	Lead by a paid professional pastor, who was educated at a seminary.
Met together in an interactive, participatory meeting.	Sing three songs and listen to one person speak in very large groups.
Entrance by repenting and being baptized.	Ask Jesus into your heart.

Father, I am so sorry for any part I have had in falsely teaching people that baptism is an option. I am sorry for supporting churches and pastors who teach that. I am sorry for any financial support or tacit approval of this false teaching. Please forgive me, Lord. I have not spoken out against this practice. I am so sorry, Father.

SEMINARIES

I know what you are thinking. "Seminaries! Surely he can't be thinking they are part of the problem. Where else would people go to study the Bible intensely? Where else would we get our pastors and missionaries?"

You know where I'm going with this. If we didn't have pastors, we wouldn't need seminaries. The paradigm is: "We must have seminaries to train pastors."

Now, I am an educator by training. I have both a bachelor of education and master of arts in teaching. I've been a lifetime teacher of sales and business principles and practices. I create and sell teaching materials.

In other words, I believe in education. So I'm favorably predisposed to approve of and encourage seminaries. Nothing wrong with a Christian education, particularly in light of the godless trend in our government-influenced high schools and colleges.

The problem is when they focus on turning out pastors. They become, then, agents to feed the system that has caused forty thousand denominations and a version of Christianity that emphasizes intellect over spirit, head over heart, correctness of doctrine over love. I'm all in favor of them educating future teachers, engineers, and business people.

However, to the degree that they shore up and feed the system, they are part of the problem.

Church of the New Testament	Institutional Church System
Lead by a plurality of elders, who are shaped by the Holy Spirit and arise out of the local church.	Lead by a paid professional pastor, who was educated at a seminary.
Met together in an interactive, participatory meeting.	Sing three songs and listen to one person speak in very large groups.

Church of the New Testament	Institutional Church System
Entrance by repenting and being baptized.	Ask Jesus into your heart.
Training by involvement with the people and the nurturing of the Holy Spirit.	Education in a seminary.

GIVING

On a recent conference call, I made a suggestion that people could use a portion of their tithes to fund an extra-church ministry. A bright, young Christian lady dismissed it out of hand by saying, "Oh no, the Bible is very clear that we are to give our tithes totally to the church." End of conversation.

Wow. The institutional church really has her. The deeply embedded paradigm, which she so unthinkingly voiced, is this: "We must give to the local congregation."

Let's look at this with an open, objective mind.

Almost all the teaching I have had from various pastors had to do with the amount to be set aside, not the act of setting it aside. My concern is not for the amount but the beneficiary of that gift.

Lest you think that my motives are base, let me tell you, with all candor, that I have the gift of giving. I enjoy it. I take personal pleasure in making anonymous gifts. For as long as I can remember, I have given at least 10 percent of my income. My income varies tremendously. So every year, at the beginning of the year, I create, with God's guidance, a giving formula for the year. As my income increases, the percentage I give goes up. It starts at 10 percent and rises in steps to 100 percent. That's right. I commit to give it all away, over and above a certain income figure. In all honesty, I have never gotten there. But I have hit multiples of 10 percent on several occasions.

Not only that, but those percentages are just of my personal income. I give the first fruits of any new business effort to the Lord from my company. On one of my websites, I give the first 15 percent of revenue—not profits, but revenue—to the work of the Lord.

My wife will tell you that I am always suggesting that we give to this or that and that she has to put a hold on me because I would have given it all away.

Not only that, but I am a generous giver of my time. I have done at least a dozen self-funded short-term mission trips to South Africa, Ghana, and Mexico, where I teach Christian business people how to grow their businesses more effectively.

I'm not saying this out of pride. I understand that my interest in giving is a spiritual gift, instilled in me by the Lord, and all the praise for it should go to him. I'm mentioning it to head off the criticism that my motives are selfish and stingy—that I really don't want to give. Quite the contrary.

So back to the question of to whom should we give it. Of course, the professional pastor system claims that money for itself. They need it, after all, to support themselves and their families and to pay for the church building. In many churches, some small portion of that is actually funneled to missions or benevolence.

Does the Bible clearly teach that our tithes should go to the local congregation, as that bright young lady asserted? Not exactly. Here's the verse that speaks to that issue most directly.

> Now about the collection for God's people. Do what I told the Galatian churches to do. On the first day of every week, each of you should set aside a sum of money in keeping with his income, saving it up, so that when I come no collection will have to be made.
>
> (1 Corinthians 16:1–2)

Notice that it is a collection "for God's people." Not "the professional Christians among us," not the "mortgage payment on our building," not "$600,000 for a new AV system for the sanctuary." The most commonly stated purpose of giving in the New Testament is to help support other Christians in dire circumstances, as was the case in this passage.

It is amazing to me that we can read the word "saving" and understand it to mean "giving." But what would happen if you did what Paul said? If you understood "saving" to mean "saving" and not "giving"? What would happen if you actually "set aside" a certain portion of your income, as you have been prospered?

On the first day of every week, you would assess how much you have been prospered that previous week and set aside a portion of that. That would mean that every time you received a paycheck or gift or financial advantage, you would put a portion of it aside so that you would have a pot of money you could use when a specific need became apparent. Isn't that exactly what Paul said?

Wouldn't you be much more personal about giving? Your gift would be a real expression of Jesus's love. You would have a personal interest it, and the contact would likely be one-to-one.

Wouldn't that be a purer use of your tithes and offerings than to mindlessly put it in the church collection and only know what it does by analyzing the quarterly financial statement?

Here's an alternate approach. I take a percentage of my income every paycheck and put it in a special checking account at our bank. We call it the give account. Then, we look for opportunities to distribute it. My position is that it is already given; we just haven't distributed it. Using that approach, we've been able to:

- Support a family in our extended family during a year of unemployment.
- Help support a couple of widows in our extended family.
- Help dozens of business people in developing countries start or expand their businesses.
- Help support a number of parachurch ministries that directly impact people.
- Help fund a dozen trips to developing countries to teach Christian business people how to grow their businesses more effectively.

I would submit that all of these are ways we can impact people for Christ in a personal, tangible way. Frankly, I'd much rather do that than support a new AV system in the sanctuary or another associate pastor.

I'm not disputing that some money should go to support those gifted teachers who labor among us. But that seems to be more theory than practice in the New Testament. We know Paul supported himself with a trade—tent making, for example. And every instance of collections being taken up were clearly one—off events designed to help brothers and sisters in need.

For example, the first recorded example of giving occurred shortly after Pentecost, when the church was new and full of power.

> All the believers were together and shared everything. They would sell their land and the things they owned and then divide the money and give it to anyone who needed it.
>
> (Acts 2:44 New Century Version)

Sounds like individual giving from one person to another to me. God is not a God of confusion. If He had wanted to, He could have said, "The believers would give to the apostles every week, and they in turn would use most of the money to support themselves and parcel out a small portion of it for those in need."

But He didn't.

Look, I have no problem with you giving money to support a gifted teacher. I do have a problem with them teaching that is the only appropriate avenue for giving. Clearly, the Bible does not teach that you should put your entire tithe into the collection plate every week. If you want to, go ahead. Just don't think that you have to. There are other ways.

Church of the New Testament	Institutional Church System
Lead by a plurality of elders, who are shaped by the Holy Spirit and arise out of the local church.	Lead by a paid professional pastor, who was educated at a seminary.
Met together in an interactive, participatory meeting.	Sing three songs and listen to one person speak in very large groups.
Entrance by repenting and being baptized.	Ask Jesus into your heart.
Training by involvement with the people and the nurturing of the Holy Spirit.	Education in a seminary.
No need for regular support. No professional clergy, no church buildings. People saved a portion of their income and gave it to other needy Christians.	Promulgates "Give your tithe to the church" in order to pay all the bills.

Church of the New Testament	Institutional Church System
Results: With no resources, penetrated the entire known world in about three hundred years, transforming millions of lives, and impacting world culture.	Results: Squandered $530 billion dollars in the last fifteen years, lost the culture, turned off half our children, divided into forty thousand different groups and inoculates most of the population from committing to Christ.

SUMMARY

We have spent 530 billion dollars, not grown a bit and lost the culture. At the same time, we have failed to grow the percentage of Christians in this country. We drive away half of our kids, we promote superficial Christianity, and we put stumbling blocks in front of millions of people who would come to Christ if it weren't for the church. This is a failure of epic proportions.

The greatest nation the world has ever known, established by Godly people on Godly principles, favored by the Almighty, has fallen. We've not managed to increase the percentage of Christians in the country, and we've allowed the culture to become immoral on its way to becoming anti-Christian. On the way, we've created mind-numbing division, lost half our children, and put obstacles to millions of people coming to Christ.

A failure this large can only come from a fault that emanates out of millions of people. What could have that much reach to impact the minds and hearts of so many people?

The institutional church system.

It is based on false principles, functions with man-made systems, and twists the clear teaching of scripture to support its own self-serving practices. In so doing it has robbed Christ's church of its resources and its power and promoted a passive, shallow form of Christianity. It stays in power through the active encouragement of a set of false paradigms. It has such a lock on people's minds that the vast majority of churchgoing Christians can't even conceive of questioning it.

> *The institutional church is based on false principles, functions with man-made systems, and twists the clear teaching of scripture to support its own self-serving practices. In so doing it has robbed Christ's church of its resources and its power, and promoted a passive, shallow form of Christianity. It stays in power through the active encouragement of a set of false paradigms. It has such a lock on people's minds that the vast majority of church-going Christians can't even conceive of questioning it.*

The lock it has on people's minds takes the form of these false paradigms, which it proclaims in all sorts of ways:

Every congregation must be led by a professional pastor.

The biblical message: There is no biblical authority for pastors. New Testament churches grow their own leaders from among them and recognize them as elders.

Going to church means attending the Sunday morning worship service. It is the heart of Christianity.

The biblical message: There is no such thing as a worship service. Followers of Christ meet in small, interactive meetings where they minister to one another and build each other up.

Every church must have its own church building.

The biblical message: Church has nothing to do with buildings. The church is the group of people who belong to Christ. This idea of church buildings is a man-made idea that has burdened millions of Christians, prevented Christian work, and siphoned off billions of dollars from the true work of the Church.

This congregation must grow!

The biblical message: It is Christ who adds to his church. We should focus on transforming our lives and those whom we disciple. Focusing on local congregational growth causes all kinds of negative consequences.

To become a Christian, just ask Jesus into your heart.

The biblical message: "Repent, and be baptized, every one of you in the name of Jesus Christ so that your sins may be forgiven. And you will receive the gifts of the Holy Spirit" (Acts 2:38). There may be no other message more plainly and repeatedly taught in the pages of the New Testament.

We must have seminaries to train pastors.

The biblical message: The Holy Spirit raises up leaders from among the church. They grow by interaction with one another and the Holy Spirit.

We must give to the local congregation.

The biblical message: We are to set aside as we have been prospered and give to those needy people to whom the Holy Spirit directs us.

The consequences are of biblical proportions. I do not claim to have the gift of prophesy. But I have studied scripture, and I am good at discerning trends and projecting them forward. Here's what I see—one person's opinion.

In the Old Testament, whenever the Israelites forsook obedience to God and turned their affection to idols, He gave them over to be conquered by a godless people who made their lives miserable. A generation or so later, they would become so miserable, they would repent and turn back to God.

We've gone beyond his patience. We're moving into the season of affliction. I see a trend in this country to just that.

Looking forward to the future, if we continue to adhere to the institutional church system, here's one person's opinion. Within the next twenty years, American democracy will be no more, and the country will be ruled by a dictator. It could be much sooner than that, even before this presidential term comes to an end. Our debt will cause us to be, on the slight end of the spectrum, heavily influenced by China. On the heavy end of the spectrum, we could be ruled by a foreign ungodly power. (Islam?)

The country will move from secular to anti-Christian. Church buildings will be taxed and confiscated. Christian institutions, from schools to hospitals, will be forced to conform to ungodly rules and give up their Christian orientation or be taxed out of existence.

At some point, the culprit will be seen to be the government and the economy, but the real problem will be spiritual—we have chosen to substitute a man-made church for God's clear and simple directions.

Christians will be persecuted, and the church will, out of necessity, move underground, into meetings in people's homes. Simple church, the way God intended it, will spread rapidly. And somewhere, two or three generations from now, if the world lasts that long, we'll get it right.

Thinking About This Chapter

Why must this congregation grow? Who benefits?

To what degree is it possible that building the local congregation is not the fulfillment of the command to "make disciples, baptizing and teaching" but rather a substitute for it?

To what degree does your congregation teach the requirement of baptism as a rite of passage into Christ's church?

Is there anywhere in the New Testament an example of the apostles or early Christians telling people to just "ask Jesus into their hearts"?

To what degree are seminaries a substitute for the work of the Holy Spirit in developing and raising up Christian leaders?

To what extent does your church teach that giving to it is a biblical mandate?

GOD'S MAJESTIC CHURCH

A number of years ago, my wife and I visited the country of Albania. This was just after the communist government had fallen, and the country was beginning to open up to the outside world. Previously, it had been the most closed and totalitarian country in the world.

We stayed in a government villa near the main square in the capital city. Each day, we had a driver and a car at our disposal. (There's quite a story behind this.) Note that at this time, there was not one stoplight in the country, because there were so few cars, there was no need for them. People walked and used ox-carts for transportation. (This was in the mid 1990s!)

Each day, we would venture out on day trips. On the way out from the villa, we would pass a crowd of people milling around the square. After a couple of days, it became obvious that many of the people were the same, day after day. When we asked the driver about it, he replied that they were standing around waiting for someone to tell them what to do.

After generations of dictatorial rule, they had lost the ability to think for themselves.

In a conversation with one of the older residents, he remarked that he felt his whole life had been wasted. "We had been told that we were the richest nation in the world," he remarked. "Now I know that we were the poorest."

By controlling the communications and feeding certain false paradigms, the established authorities controlled the population. The people were focused internally and believed what they were told. It wasn't until the country opened up, and they could see their world from the outside, that the truth of their poverty became apparent.

I am afraid that many Christians are in a similar situation. Held in check by the ubiquitous teaching and the false paradigms of the institutional church system, we cannot see it for what it is because we are so deeply embedded in the inside of it.

The institutional church system is not the church. No matter what the established professionals claim, God is much bigger than just this man-made construction.

Understanding that Christ's church is not defined by the denominational rules, nor the attendance in an ICS worship service, nor the official membership of a local congregation; rather it is defined by the all those people who Christ has added to his church. Of this larger, worldwide population, it is my belief that the ICS now houses a minority of Christians in this country. In other words, there are more Christians who are outside of the ICS than there are inside.

In speaking engagements, I'll ask the audience this question, "How many of you know at least one non-IC church Christians?"

If everyone knows at least one, then using just this simple indicator, the number of non-IC Christians, is at least as big as the number of IC adherents.

The church of Christ is not just those regular churchgoers. It is everyone who has heeded the biblical mandate to "repent, and be baptized." There are at least as many outside the ICS as there are inside.

Jesus is present, to edify and nurture his people, wherever "two or three are gathered" in His name (Matt 18:20). Thus church meetings don't just happen on Sunday morning inside buildings; they happen in all sorts of circumstances and settings.

Once you get outside of the ICS, you see God at work everywhere. When you have coffee with a believer, you are promised that "Where two or three are gathered in my name, there I am." In other words, that is a meeting of the church. When you have lunch with a fellow Christian or meet for a Bible study or just share some time together, that is a meeting of the church. God's church and His spirit is everywhere. But that is very difficult to see as long as we are on the inside.

If you are seriously considering the positions discussed in this book, you are probably confronting what is, for each of us, a huge issue. It's the practical issue. If you don't do church in the traditional, institutional sense, what do you do? How do you fill that void next Sunday?

While I may not have the solution for next Sunday, I can certainly point you in a direction that will help fill the void somewhere down the road. God has not vacated the premises. There are options.

First, understand that you are not alone and that your new and clarified understanding of the church is not a radical or unique idea. You are part of a trend as old as the church itself. In every generation, in every country where people have had access to the scriptures, they have come to the same conclusions:

- Baptism of adult believers is commanded as a rite of initiation in the church.
- The Lord's Supper should be practiced weekly.
- Meetings should be interactive.
- There should be no greater organization than the local congregation.

Throughout history, individuals and groups, reading the Bible without the interpretation of professional Christians, have come to these positions, over and over, in every generation. At times, they have tried to reform the institutional church system and always failed. At other times, they have gone off on their own and tried to separate themselves from it. They were routinely persecuted for doing so. History is full of torture and murder—sometimes mass murders—by the institutional church in power at the moment, as they tried to stifle those who found fault with it.

If you are interested in digging deeper into this issue, read E. H. Broadbent's landmark book *The Pilgrim Church*, originally published in 1931. In it he traces the history of the alternative church from the time of the apostles to modern times.

What is different about our times and our generation is that the Lord has given us a great window of opportunity to unleash the Holy Spirit and return the church to its roots and its power. At the moment, in Western civilization, we don't need to fear persecution from the institutional church system. The local pastor of the congregation you left is probably not going to get the authorities to arrest you; he's not going to burn down your home, destroy your businesses, and attack your families.

Probably the worst that will happen to you is that the professional Christians will question your salvation, call you a heretic, and accuse you of being hateful. You can live with that.

So you have an opportunity to connect with God and get church right which, in the history of the church, is almost unique. Few generations, over the past two thousand years, have been able to operate with such freedom from persecution. The time is right, the need is great, and the Lord wants you! To quote the words of Mordecai to Ester, "Who knows but that you have come to this position for such as time as this?" (Ester 5:14)

In the chapter "Where to from Here?" I list some of the books, websites, and organizations who support this cause. For now, let's consider some existing options.

HOUSE CHURCHES

There is a rapidly growing movement to return to the New Testament pattern of meeting in smaller groups in people's houses. Supporting that movement is a body of work by a number of authors (listed later), websites, and organizations.

The problem is, of course, locating them. They aren't listed in the yellow pages, as are the institutional churches. So if you don't mind the looks of incredulousness on the part of most of your friends, start asking around. Chances are, someone knows someone who is involved in a house church. Two websites that may be of value are House Church Central and House2House (see chapter "Where to from Here?"). Both of these have directories of house churches and contain lots of information to get you acquainted with the concept.

House churches come in all kinds of flavors and variations. Generally though they have these characteristics in common.

1. Small group. The size is usually limited to the space of the living room or basement where the group meets.
2. Interactive. They really do try to follow Paul's commands in 1 Corinthians 14 for "each one." You'll notice a degree of respect for each individual and their unique contribution to the group you may not have seen before.
3. Pastor-less. Some will have people who manage the group, facilitate the meetings, and may even

bring more formal lessons. Some have no one like that. Regardless, it's a rare house church that has a person who comes close to having the central position of the institutional church pastors.

Beyond that, they vary. Having a meal together is central to many house churches, as was the pattern in the New Testament. The Lord's Supper may be a totally new experience for you. (Not many little round wafers and gold-plated cups here.)

What you likely will find is dialogue more honest and refreshing than you may have ever experienced, real relationships, prayers much more personal and intense than those in the worship services with which you may be familiar, and a conspicuous lack of format.

House churches are growing rapidly all over the world. In China, the vast majority of Christians meet in house churches. They may be one of the reasons for the rapid growth of Christianity in that country. It may be that there are more Christians in China (estimated at about 159 million) than any other country in the world.[22] That is the natural outcome of a church that has been forced to meet the way God intended it to meet. Who *knows* what would have happened if the institutional church were allowed to freely operate in China. I can speculate—anemic growth, superficial Christians, and rampant division.

Just recently there was an international dustup over an American Christian who was jailed in Iran for being involved with house churches. A friend of mine, who is in a position to know, indicated to me that there were fifty thousand house churches in Iran. It seems God's undercover movement is alive and well in at least one Muslim nation.

As this practice of simple church continues to grow, it's likely to be seen more and more as a viable alternative by more and more of the traditional, institutional Christians. George Barna projected that somewhere between 3 percent and 22 percent of the adult population in this country has at least some experience with house churches.[23]

In my own journey, we moved away from the institutional church in stages. First, we left the church where I had been an elder and Bible school teacher. We spent a couple of years visiting other churches. We'd light on one for a few weeks and then grow discouraged and move on. We probably visited a couple of dozen institutional churches and found none of them, from the small congregations made up of a few families to the mega-churches of thousands, to fill the void we were feeling in our spiritual lives.

Gradually, I came to see that house churches really were God's pattern. So we looked for house churches. Our search uncovered three or four. We visited each and found them to be much more in sync with our growing understanding of the Lord's church. There were always issues though that prevented our joining one. Generally, they were all too distant. We were not going to drive forty-five to sixty minutes every week to be a part of one.

Eventually, I came to the conclusion that if we were going to be a part of a house church, I was going to have to start one. This was a major realization for me, prompted, I'm sure, by the Spirit. My position at this point was that I never wanted to be in a leadership capacity in the church again, as I was still smarting from my experience as an elder.

I had to let that position go if I was going to move forward. After much prayer, Coleen and I decided to start a house church. We passed the word to some friends, made some connections on the Internet, and put together a motley crew of Christians who gathered together in our living room to experiment with this radical concept.

For the next five or six years, we met with this small group of Christians. Our youngest daughter was raised in this environment and knew it as her church. To this day, I attribute her exceptional level of spiritual sensitivity and maturity to her involvement with our house church, as opposed to the institutions which her older siblings knew as church.

During this time, I became associated with Open Church Ministries, a nonprofit group that grew up around the success of *The Open Church* book by Jim Rutz. It was originally conceived as a ministry to encourage and stimulate open churches, which we interpreted as house churches. As Michigan coordinators, Coleen and I organized and hosted a couple of statewide conferences and would visit with groups or individuals anywhere in the state who expressed an interest in starting a house church.

Alas, the national ministry was eventually turned over to a more traditional pastor, and the emphasis on local support disappeared. My travel schedule became more and more demanding, and our house church became a casualty of my being unable to attend consistently.

In retrospect, it was a period of great growth for Coleen, Kelly, and me. The relationships we formed with our brothers and sisters have maintained to this day. We really and truly did *help each other get through life*. And those relationships and attachments continue to this day.

MARKETPLACE MINISTRIES

Once we free ourselves of the cultural paradigms which say the church is only in a building overseen by a pastor, we then open up the possibilities of seeing that God is everywhere, and church is wherever "two or three are gathered together in my name."

One such place in which God is showing up in a more powerful and pervasive movement is the marketplace. Christian business people are searching for, and finding, the things which the institutional church was never able to provide them: Fellowship with like-minded people, application of biblical truths to their situations and challenges, Spirit-led interactions with others, and a sense of purpose and usefulness—a place where their gifts, education, and experience are appreciated and demanded as central to God's work.

> *Christian business people are searching for, and finding, the things which the institutional church was never able to provide them: Fellowship with like-minded people, application of biblical truths to their situations and challenges, Spirit-led interactions with others, and a sense of purpose and usefulness – a place where their gifts, education and experience are appreciated and demanded as central to God's work.*

While there have been organizations in this space for generations, God has been far more active in recent years providing, among other things, an alternative to church. The Christian Business Men's Connection has long provided Christian business people a marketplace-oriented opportunity to fellowship with one another, pray and study together, and collaborate for evangelism and discipleship. The Christian Chamber of Commerce has provided a forum for networking and support for Christian business owners.

While these mainstays have been around for decades, the new movement of God has raised up a multiple of other resources. Os Hillman's *Today God Is First* daily devotional for Christian business people goes to over one hundred thousand opt-in subscribers every day, for example.[24]

Indianapolis-based Truth@Work reaches across the country to provide a structured monthly meeting, much like an advisory board of advisors and an online library of curriculum designed to help Christian business owners and executives run their businesses and their lives in a more godly way.

As a Truth@Work chapter president, I organize and facilitate groups of Christian business people in these monthly meetings. And while we don't call it church, our meetings clearly are that—like-minded people getting together in Jesus's name to help one another live more Godly lives and run more Godly businesses. In many ways, our meetings are more "church" the way God intended it to be than the typical worship services of the institutional church.

In addition, there are other such organizations, both national and local. Websites are popping up all over the place, and God is raising gifted leaders to impact the workplace for him.

If you are a Christian business person looking for a more impactful experience of his church, I suspect there are multiple marketplace options in your community.

That God should be working in special ways within the marketplace should come as no surprise to the biblical scholar. Almost every major movement of God has been led by a business person. Let's consider them:

- *Abraham:* As God moved to set aside a chosen people for His covenant, He chose a wealthy farmer/rancher to do the work.
- *Joseph:* Moving God's fledging people to Egypt so that they could multiply, it was Joseph, a business person who ran the pharaoh's food distribution system, whom God picked to facilitate this critical movement.

- *Moses:* Royally raised and educated but a shepherd by vocation, Moses led the Israelites to the Promised Land.
- *Nehemiah:* After the captivity, God chose an executive in the king's court to supervise the rebuilding of the city and the organization of God's people as they reestablished themselves.
- *Jesus:* A carpenter who made his living in the marketplace; he probably was a small business owner, making furniture and maybe homes for people, prior to the full-time pursuit of his ministry.
- *Paul:* A lifetime craftsman; he was a tentmaker, probably in sole-proprietorship, who supported himself and much of his travels in the marketplace.

While house churches and the business as mission movement are two rapidly growing expressions of God's presence and power, they certainly aren't the only places God is making himself known in new and more powerful ways. They just happen to be the two that are closest to me.

Extra-church Ministries

I see a rapid growth in ministries that are not associated with any church but which attempt to address some need in the world with Christian compassion and resources. I call them extra-church ministries, with "extra" meaning outside of the institutional church system. In the light of the IC system's dismal failure at evangelizing the country, impacting the culture, unleashing the saints' spiritual gifts, or equipping people for works of service, God has not been sitting on the sidelines. He's stimulated and nurtured literally thousands of nonprofit ministries to actually do the work that the ICS has not done. It seems that every week I come across another one.

In almost every conceivable area, if you have an issue, a need, or an interest, there are probably a choice of ministries with which you can become involved. Ministries for men, or women, for teens, for missions, for benevolence, etcetera—the list goes on almost without end. If you want to be involved in works of service, you are probably just a Google search away for connecting with a ministry focusing on your area of interest.

I suspect that as the culture sinks deeper and deeper into an anti-Christian mind-set, we'll see him evidence himself in new and exciting ways.

Thinking About This Chapter

To what degree is it possible that you have some erroneous paradigms regarding the church?

How many non-churched (ICS version) Christians do you know?

Is it possible that there are more Christians outside of the ICS then inside?

How many house church Christians do you know? How could make a connection with a house church in the next few weeks?

What Christian marketplace ministries are available in your location? What would have to happen for you to connect with one of them in the next few weeks?

To what degree are their extra-church ministries operating in areas in which you have interest or gifting? How could you connect with one or more that resonated with your passions?

WHAT HAPPENS WHEN THERE IS NO PASTOR?

A CASE STUDY

It's hard to imagine that a congregation could function without a pastor. It wouldn't really be a church, would it? Actually, it may surprise you. Here's my story.

In 1984, I was transferred from the metro-Detroit area to Grand Rapids to take a promotion. We moved our family, settled into a neighborhood on the north side of the city, and began to look for a church.

We found a small, nondenominational church in a semirural setting not too far from home. It was a small, traditional church with a long history, having been in that location for generations. But the people were friendly and the pastor charismatic. The congregation was growing, and they welcomed us with open arms.

We soon became immersed in the needs of the congregation. I began teaching the adult Sunday school class, and Coleen, my wife, began assisting with crises counseling, one of her gifts.

Very soon after, I was approached by the pastor to become one of the elders, joining two other men in that position. After some reluctance, I agreed and was appointed by the congregation.

From the inside, I began to see some cracks in the veneer. The pastor had a grudge against one of the elders, whom he felt had wronged him in some real estate transaction a few years earlier. He did his best to avoid the elder and tried never to talk to him.

I began to notice some unilateral decisions and high-handed behavior on the part of the pastor. He verbalized that he considered himself the chief elder and was the hub of the wheel around which everything revolves. We invited him to join with us, the three elders, to work out some rules and organization among us. He refused to meet with us because of his disdain for my colleague.

The three elders went off for a retreat weekend. At that meeting, we created some guidelines and rules for the division of labor and responsibility among us.

We then asked the pastor to meet with us to discuss our work. At that meeting, he announced, out of the blue, that we are going to witness a family event. Either we could see the birth of a new church or a nasty divorce. It was up to us to decide.

He had been scheming and manipulating in the background, gathering a group of people to follow him in the creation of a new congregation. A few days, later he was gone, along with about one-third of the congregation.

At the time, I was shocked (where did this come from?), perplexed (wow did this happen?), and over-whelmed (why me?). I recall thinking that this phenom-enon of church splits lead by disgruntled senior pastors was generally a disease that primarily afflicted the par-ticular religious body with which I was then affiliated.

Since then I've learned that not to be true. Within a few weeks of the event, I discovered an acquaint-ance who had lived through an almost identical situ-ation in his Presbyterian church. Next I learned of a large independent congregation not far from us that had gone through an amazingly similar situation a few years earlier.

So on Thursday, we met with the pastor. Three days later, one-third of the congregation was gone, as was one of the other elders and the pastor.

The other elder and I were left with about eighty people, a hundred-year-old building, and not a clue as to what to do.

We could have, I suppose, taken the easy way out. Regrouped, hired a new pastor, and went about our business.

Following a lot of prayer, we elected a different course of action. We decided that this sudden shift in the life and organization of the congregation really pre-sented an opportunity to do it right. So we elected to study the scriptures and see if we could get some guid-ance from them. What we discovered, I have described

above in the previous chapters. Coming to the scriptures without any preconceived notions, with no seminary instruction to cloud our views and obscure our
understanding, we concluded that the position of paid
pastor was nowhere found in the New Testament.

We did see evangelists, elders, teachers, prophets,
and apostles described. We concluded that the elders
were clearly the folks responsible for the health and
well-being of the congregation, under the headship of
Christ and empowered by the Holy Spirit. We knew
we had to have teachers and believed that we should
support an evangelist.

We wrote up a position paper (see attachment 1)
and sought to find an evangelist to support. To this day,
I remember very odd (or so it seems to me) conversations with the men we interviewed. Of the six or seven
that we interviewed, everyone said, "Yes. Your position
is absolutely correct. That is what the New Testament
teaches. But it won't work in this culture." To this
day, I find it incredible that these, supposedly men of
God, were saying that God's word was unworkable in
our society.

Eventually we found a man who not only agreed
with our position but was eager to serve as a full-
time evangelist, seeing that as his primary gifting. We
brought him into the congregation as a full-time, fully
supported evangelist.

During this time, we had developed a routine. I
would bring the message from the pulpit on the average of once a month. Another member of the congregation who was a former pastor did likewise once a

month, and on the other two Sundays of each month,
we'd generally have someone from outside the congregation fill in: Missionaries on furlough, representatives
from para-church ministries, an occasional pastor from
a local congregation. I found it exhilarating, and the
diversity of perspectives brought a fresh air into the
congregation. I recall one Sunday being impressed
with the power of the Holy Spirit working in the lives
of young men from Teen Challenge as they shared
their testimonies.

On some occasions, we would have members of the
congregation share the pulpit. I remember one Mother's
Day, when the sermon time was filled by seven or eight
women from the congregation, each speaking of their
reflections and insights into being a mother and having mothers.

We decided to continue that practice, reasoning that
if we had the evangelist speak, the congregation would
begin to see him as the pastor, a situation we were
afraid to encourage. Further, our understanding of the
way God had organized His church indicated that the
elders were responsible for the family of God, while the
evangelist's first responsibility was to the lost. Since the
Sunday services were almost exclusively those who had
already been saved, that made them our responsibility,
not the evangelist. So he and his family sat in the pews,
as would every other member of the congregation.

This continued for over a year. The results were
remarkable. In that time frame, over one hundred people were brought to the Lord and baptized. The congregation, seeing that there was no paid pastor to do their

work for them, stepped up. At one point, we calculated that we had 90 percent of the adults in the congregation active in some ministry effort. People found needs and stepped up to fill them. There was a spirit of unity and enthusiasm in the church.

It was a case study of what could happen when there was no pastor, and the congregation attempted to carry on without one.

Alas, it didn't last. It seemed the old guard in the congregation was never really comfortable with the pastor-less model. I remember several continually asking, "When are we going to have a leader?" Their constant mumbling and lobbying for a leader combined with my family's growing interest in missionary work in South Africa. Eventually, we gave in, stepped down, moved out of the congregation, and the evangelist, who had once been so enthusiastic about his role, stepped in as de facto pastor.

Over the next few years, the spirit of unity left the church, and the sense of ownership and community began to dissolve. The number of people brought to the Lord slowed to a trickle, and a few years later, the church split again.

I have attached transcriptions of the documents that we created. I have elected to remove the names of people and the congregation to spare them the scrutiny that I expect will follow.

In retrospect, our noble experiment only extended so far. We continued to have worship services, for example, instead of church meetings. We continued to encourage giving to the congregation.

If I were in that same situation today, knowing what I know now, I would not have attempted to reform that local congregation, understanding that the institutional church paradigms are so deeply embedded into the psyche of western Christians that real change, change in the system, is so big that it is only achieved by a movement of God. I would have left much sooner than I did.

Thinking About This Chapter

What would happen if you attempted to meet with other Christians in a church setting without a pastor?

What would happen if your congregation fully supported an evangelist?

To what degree do you think it is possible to reform the institutional church system?

Is your most promising course of action not to attempt to reform it but rather just to leave it?

WHERE TO
FROM HERE?

I s the institutional church really the church?

While it may be spiritually impotent, it does have some utility. For someone wanting to connect with other local Christians, it serves as a type of holy country club, where the dues are voluntary and the expectations are manageable. It is a place where you can connect with other Christians in similar places in their lives. For almost every stage of your life, if you select the church wisely, you'll find Christians that share your issues.

In the age of social media though, I wonder about the utility of investing time and energy in a church just for the purpose of socialization. I suspect that one of the reasons such a large percentage of our young people leave the church has to do with the ease of connecting on Facebook and other social media sites. When it is so easy to connect with your peers on social media with the ubiquitous cell phone, who needs the youth group? Is it possible that the institutional church will fall victim to social media?

In addition to the social aspects of the institutional church, there is some advantage to the buying power of the institutional church. By grouping the buying power of the congregation together, it can do things that are difficult for individuals to do on their own. It can organize mission trips, for example, arrange for marriage counseling, and put on first class entertainment concerts, to name a few.

However, just a little bit of effort will uncover a selection of nonprofit organizations who can arrange for a mission trip for you and your teenagers, provide marriage counseling, sponsor entertainment experiences, and do just about everything that we think of being within the province of the local congregation.

A great model has been established by the folks in the home school movement. I marvel that they have been able to field athletic teams, organize field trips, and provide for superior education with a fraction of the resources of the public school system. Maybe there is a lesson there for those looking for an alternative to the institutional church system.

Beyond that, I'm not sure what other practical utility the local congregation provides. As a spiritual entity, it certainly is irrelevant to the majority of the US population who view it with disdain. It frames their views of what Christianity is and projects an image that is distasteful and irrelevant to their lives. Clearly, the church of Jesus Christ would not be so negatively viewed. Maybe the ICS is not really the church.

It's impotent to the vast majority of Christians who go through the motions of church attendance and are content with the superficial Christianity which is the result of years of church. These folks rarely grow spiritually beyond the "milk" stage, look at the pastor to do the work for them, and are content to live their lives without any significant spiritual component to them. It may be something to do for the vast majority of Christians, but it is clearly does not have the impact on people that the church of Christ had. Maybe the ICS is not really the church.

It's frustrating to those Christians who know there is something bigger and deeper for them spiritually but are quietly frustrated with the church's lack of ability to provide it. They don't know what to do, but they sense that their church will not get them to a higher level. Maybe the ICS is not really the church.

It's a hindrance to the millions of young people who have been, and will be, raised to think of the institution as Christ's body and yet are so unequipped by it and uninvolved with it that they reject it as soon as they leave home. They find it irrelevant but have nothing to take its place. Maybe the ICS is not really the church.

It's irrelevant, I suspect, to you. Maybe the ICS is not really the church.

I don't presume to know where you are in your spiritual journey. Some of you are no doubt angry with me, consider me a heretic, an enemy of the church, and are even plotting ways to silence my message and discredit me.

For others, the cultural paradigms are so deeply attached to your image of yourself that, while you may understand them intellectually, you can't possibly question or let go of them emotionally.

Others agree with my observations but are puzzled about how to move forward, and so deeply intertwined with the institution that you'll find yourself unable to act on your new convictions.

Still others see the world in a similar way to that which I described. There's a part of you that is angry with the institution for robbing you of the relationship with Christ you could have had, for boring and turning off your kids, for squandering your contributions, for inoculating millions of people from committing to Christ.

There is probably a handful of you that are ready to take drastic action now. You are convinced that the ICS is not really the church.

Wherever you are in your spiritual journey, I hope to have prodded you to reexamine the paradigms, which I believe have kept you captive. I hope we have pried some of those screens off the box, which damped the light of the Spirit within you.

But you must do something. Doing nothing—maintaining the status quo—is unfortunately no longer a viable option. We cannot any longer make excuses for the church and go along with the program. By doing that we contribute to the fruits of the institutional church system: 530 billion dollars, no growth, unthinkable division, lost children, and a lost culture.

One of my friends recently voiced this position. "Yes, the institutional church is a man-made institution, and nothing like the picture in the New Testament. But it's all we have, and we have to work with it. Everyone has flaws, including the church."

I must confess that for years, I accepted that position. Not anymore.

We've lost the culture, squandered 530 billion dollars, and are at risk of losing the nation totally. We've accepted sinful division, we're losing our children, and we're turning off millions who could come to Christ if we would remove the stumbling blocks. Making compromises with a man-made system is no longer acceptable. Enough is enough.

> *We've lost the culture, squandered 530 billion dollars and are at risk of losing the nation totally. We've accepted sinful division, we're losing our children, and we're turning off millions who could come to Christ if we would remove the stumbling blocks. Making compromises with a man-made system is no longer acceptable. Enough is enough!*

There are a number of other positions on the spectrum of possible actions. One possible approach is to believe that God is raising alternatives to the institutional church system all around you. Decide to look for them in your community. Begin looking for a house church. It may take some time, but the movement is growing daily, and there is bound to be an option near you. As an alternative, consider talking to your small group about becoming a house church.

Look for other ways of connecting with like-minded Christians. If you are a business person, investigate CBMC, Truth@Work, and the other similar organizations.

Turn to the Lord, pray fervently that He will direct you to a connection with other Christians. Don't have preconceived notions that it must be a church. Expect that He will lead you to a more intense involvement with Him, and be open enough to follow His leading.

Stop supporting the institution financially. Do something different with your tithes and donations. If just 20 percent of the folks who attend institutional churches would remove their tithes and channel those resources to people's needs in a direct and personal way, that may, by itself, be enough to cause a turn in the culture.

At some point, you will have to disengage. You'll need to walk away. You will not reform the institution from within. The power of the institution, in the big picture, will not allow you to do it. You may have some small local victories, but the institution is powerful because it eventually pressures conformity to its paradigms. You will not be successful in reforming it from within.

You will not convince a pastor who has been trained in a seminary, who makes his living by preaching every Sunday, to think differently. You will not convince a congregation that just mortgaged a new building that they should break into house churches. You will not convince a pastor who is growing in political visibility in his denomination that the denominational infrastructure is a misappropriation of the Lord's resources.

As Broadbent points out in his book *The Pilgrim Church*, every attempt to reform the institutional church from within has failed—generation after generation for two thousand years. Let's learn from those who have gone before us and not repeat their mistakes.

At some point, you will need to walk away.

One of the things that I have learned is that before you can say yes to something, you must say no to that thing that holds you back and occupies your time. *No* precedes and allows for *yes*. At some point, you will need to walk away. The Lord's church is operating outside of the walls of the institutional church. Let the Lord deal with the system. Find and connect with the alternative.

I suspect that a few years from now, you'll look at your decision to walk away from the institutional church system as one of the best decisions you will have made, ushering in a new season of spiritual growth for you and your family.

A Thirty-Day Transformation

If you are convinced that there is a greater and deeper spiritual experience awaiting you outside of the fetters or the ICS, if you are more inpatient with halfway steps and want to escape the paradigms that have been holding you back, you can be totally free and into a new plane of spirituality within a month. Here's how:

Week 1

1. Have a conversation with your spouse and family, and get everyone focused on the new agenda.
2. Spend the first week in prayer, in every way, time, and means possible.

Week 2

3. Decide to hold a church meeting in your home, with your family, on a date you determine—about three weeks from now.
4. Invite extended family and some friends to join with you.
5. Visit your bank and set up a new checking account, into which you'll deposit your "give-savings."
6. Stop giving to the ICS, and instead, deposit into your new "giving" account.
7. Give your family the responsibility to identify needs for financial gifts in the communities in which they are active.

Week 3

8. Do a Google search for ministries that you, your family, or individual family members could be involved. Reach out to several, and see which resonate with you; begin the process of getting involved.

Week 4

9. Hold your first family/friend church meeting in your home. Follow the guidelines in 1 Corinthians 14.
10. Now, focus on making disciples.

> All power in heaven and on earth is given to me. So go and make disciples of all nations, baptizing them in the name of the Father and of the Son and of the Holy Spirit, and teaching them to obey everything I have commanded you. And surely I will be with you always, to the very end of the age.
>
> (Matthew 28:18–20)

Jesus did not say, "Go and plant churches." He said, go and make disciples. It is God who adds people to His church. If you focus on making disciples, God will naturally bring them together in groups to encourage and edify each other. He calls these groups His church.

The ultimate solution is to focus on making disciples and let Him take care of His church.

Understand that you are a work in progress—it is not going to be smooth, probably not well organized and not programmed. That's okay. Remember, "When two or three are gathered in my name, there I am." Just focus on building each other up, on ministering to one another. Relax, this is Christ's church.

In a month, you could be in an exciting new place spirituality. You would be meeting as a church, in your household. You would have elevated the practice of giving to a family wide, very personal level. You would have connected with some ministries with some exciting works of service to which you can be a part. You would have vaulted out of the ICS and into a whole new level of spirituality for you and your family. You journey has begun.

Thinking About This Chapter

How important is the social aspect of your local congregation to you?

Is it possible that you substitute a more active social media presence for it?

How important is the buying power of the institutional church to you?

Is it possible that you could substitute a relationship with a variety of nonprofit enterprises for it?

To what degree do you sense that there is something bigger and deeper in Christianity for you, but you have been unable to find it?

To what degree are your actions constrained by the paradigms discussed in this book?

What will change if you do nothing?

To what degree do you think that enough is enough?

Are you ready to split from the Institutional Church System?

What would prevent you from implementing the one month spiritual transformation?

RESOURCES FOR
THE JOURNEY

I am hardly the first person to have seen and alerted people to these issues. Rather I'm only one in a long line of thinkers and writers who have, for generations, observed and expanded upon similar themes. You may recall a quote, in the chapter "It's Our Fault" of a work written in 1865, for example. As E. H. Broadbent points out, in *The Pilgrim Church*, originally written in 1931, there is a long history of a movement toward "simple, organic church," which has arisen in every place and in every generation that had access to the scriptures. In recent years, the Lord has been more active in raising up people to give voice to these "alternative" views, pushing them more and more into our consciousness, and moving them to widespread acceptance.

What follows is a sampling of some of the resources that the Lord has scattered among us. It is not meant as an exhaustive listing but rather as places to get started. The themes of this book—the de-Christianization of the culture, the failure of the institutional church, God raising up alternatives in the form of house churches, the growing understanding of work as worship, and the rise of groups of business people—are all becoming movements. Truly God is at work in these areas. The listing of resources that follows is my attempt to capture a sense of the depth and breadth of these movements.

I'm sure that this list will be somewhat obsolete by the time you read this. That's okay, because it illustrates the point that with just a little bit of open-minded searching, you can uncover a plethora of possibilities.

My apologies to the army of other authors and thought leaders who have created similar works for not including yours in this list. No slight is intended. These just happen to be those that I have person- ally encountered.

THE DE-CHRISTIANIZATION OF THE CULTURE

Books

1. Cahn, Jonathan. 2011. *The Harbinger.* Lake Mary, Florida: Frontline Charisma Media. Charisma House Book Group.
2. Enlow, Johnny. 2008. *The Seven Mountain Prophecy: Unveiling the Coming Elijah Revolution.* Lake Mary, Florida: Creation House
3. Draughon, Wells Earl. 2007. *While America Sleeps, How Islam, Immigration and Indoctrination are Destroying America from Within.* Lincoln, NE: iUniverse

4. Gunn, Colin, and Fernandez, Joaquin. 2012. *Indoctrination, Public Schools and the Decline of Christianity.* Green Forest, AR: Master Books

5. Kupelian, David. 2005. *The Marketing of Evil. How Radicals, Elitists and Pseudo-Experts Sell Us Corruption Disguised as Freedom.* Nashville, TN: Cumberland House Publishing, Inc.

6. Kinnaman, David.²011. *You Lost Me. Why Young Christians are Leaving Church….*Grand Rapids, MI: Baker Books.

Website

7. Google 2011 http://www.theharbinger-jonathancahn.com/

THE FAILURE OF THE INSTITUTIONAL CHURCH

Books

8. Knapp, John C. 2012 *How the Church Fails Businesspeople.* Grand Rapids, MI: William B. Erdmans Publishing Company

9. Wagner, C. Peter. 2005 *Freedom from the Religious Spirit.* Venture, CA: Regal Books

10. Chan, Francis, and Sprinkle, Preston. 2011. *Erasing Hell.* Colorado Springs, CO: David C. Cook.

11. Hebert, Teryl. *The Biblical Church, Bringing the Teaching of Jesus and Biblical Community into Your Home*. 2011. Sheridan books.
12. Loosley, Ernest 1935. *When the Church Was Young*. Edited and revised Sargent. GA: The Seed Sowers.
13. Viola, Frank, and Barna, George. 2002, 2008. *Pagan Christianity*. Tyndale House Publishers, Inc.
14. Rutz, James H. 1992. *The Open Church*. Auburn, ME: The Seed Sowers.
15. Kinnaman, David and Lyone, Gabe. 2007. *unchristian*. Baker Books.
16. Broadbent, E. H., original release in 1931, new edition, 2013. *The Pilgrim Church*. Gospel Folio Press.

THE GROWING HOUSE CHURCH MOVEMENT

Books

17. Edited by Atkerson, Steve. 1996. *Toward a House Church Theology*. Atlanta, GA: New Testament Restoration Foundation
18. Edited by Atkerson, Steve. 2005. *ekklesia, To the Roots of Biblical House Church Life*. Atlanta, GA: New Testament Restoration Foundation
19. Krupp, Nate. 1993. *God's Simple Plan for His Church, and Your Place in It*. Woodburn, OR: Solid Rock Books

20. Edwards, Gene. 1993. *How to Meet Under the Headship of Jesus Christ.* Beaumont, TX: Message Ministry.

Websites

21. House Church Central: http://www.hccentral. com/index.html. This is a great starting point for all things house church.
22. House2House: http://www.site.house2house. com/ This organization proactively promotes house churches. Another great starting point.

The Growing Understanding of Work As Worship and the Rise of Groups of Business People

Books

23. DeKoster, Lester. 1982. Second Edition. 2010 *Work, The Meaning of Your Life; A Christian Perspective.* Grand Rapids, MI: Christian's Library Press.
24. Rundle, Steve, and Steffen, Tom. 2003. *Great Commission Companies: The Emerging Role of Business in Missions.* Downers Grove, IL: InterVarsity Press.
25. Seebeck, Doug, and Stoner, Timothy. 2009. *My Business My Mission: Fighting Poverty Through Partnerships.* Grand Rapids, MI: Partners Worldwide.

26. Veith, Gene Edward Jr. 2002. *God at Work.* Wheaton, IL: Crossway Books.
27. Stevens, Paul R. 2002. *The Other Six Days: Vocation, Work, and Ministry in Biblical Perspective.* Grand Rapids, MI: William C. Erdmanns
28. Marshal, Rich. 2000. *GOD @ Work.* Shippensburg, PA: Destiny Image Publishers.
29. Sherman, Doug, and Hendricks, William. 1987. *Your Work Matters to God.* Colorado Springs, CO: NavPress.
30. Fraser, Robert. 2006. *Marketplace Christianity: Discovering the Kingdom Purpose of the Marketplace.* Overland Park, KS: New Grid Publishing.
31. Eldred, Ken. 2005. *God is at Work: Transforming People and Nations Through Business.* Ventura, CA: Regal Books.
32. Tsukahira, Peter. 2000. *My Father's Business: Guidelines for Ministry in the Marketplace.*
33. Blackaby, Henry, and Blackaby, Richard. 2008 *God in the Market Place.* Nashville, TN: B&H Publishing Group.
34. Hillman, Os. 2005. *The 9 to 5 window: How faith can transform the workplace.* Ventura, CA: Regal Books.

Websites

35. Daily emailed devotional—TGIF—Today God is First by Os Hillman: http://www.marketplaceleaders.org/tgif/

36. Truth@Work Christian Roundtables: http://www.christianroundtablegroups.com/public/default.asp.

37. Christian Business Men's Connection: http://www.cbmc.com/.

38. A Call to Arms for Christian Business people: http://www.acalltoarms.co.

39. Ezine for Christian business people: http://www.acalltoarms.co

APPENDIX

ATTACHMENT 1

The First of Our Organizational Documents:
A Transcription of Our Position Paper

The Evangelist

What Kind of Man?

We (the members of the evangelist procurement committee) have a vision of what the future can hold for xxxxxxxxxxxxxxxxxxxxx. Obviously, the man that is selected to be the evangelist of this congregation will have a very key role in fulfilling that vision. Therefore, there are certain characteristics that we will be looking for as we interview, investigate background, listen to messages and review resumes.

Some of the issues to which we are sensitive are:

- What priority does the prospective evangelist give to the church's outreach program?
- How does he define the role of the evangelist in that outreach effort?

- Does he equate the delivery of "sermons" with evangelism and preaching?
- What proportionate ratio of his time should be spent on counseling?

These are not trick questions but are critical to our understanding of the evangelist's personal career objectives; and they are critical to helping him know what we expect of him.

From extensive examination of the word of God, we have found the word "evangelist" to be a transliteration of a word in the Greek language which really means "one who gives good news", or, "a good newser."

Paul tells Timothy to "*do the work of an evangelist* (or 'be a good newser')". In the books of I Timothy, II Timothy and Titus, we learn just what it meant to do that work. Among other things, it included *"Preach the word; be prepared in season and out of season; correct, rebuke and encourage...Do the work of an evangelist"* (II Timothy 4:2, 5)

In the book of Acts, Phillip is referred to as "the evangelist", or "good newser" (Acts 21:8) after having labored in Samaria where many people *"believed Philip as he preached the good news of the kingdom of God and the name of Jesus Christ...(and) were baptized, both men and women"*. (Acts 8:12)

We also recall that it was Phillip that joined himself to the chariot of the queen's treasurer from Ethiopia and *"told him the good news about Jesus"* (Acts 8:35). Later this same evangelist, Phillip, appears at Azotus *"preaching the good news in all the towns until he reached Caesarea"*. (Acts 8:40)

We infer from the above scriptures that the preponderance of the evangelist's work is intensely concentrated on sharing the message of salvation—available through the death, burial and resurrection of Jesus Christ (I Cor. 15:1–4)—with the non-Christian. Plain and simple. That's it. There is no other priority! The conversion of the lost and the gathering of those thus saved into worshipping communities (local congregations) is the sum total of the duties of the evangelist.

Of course, in the wake of the immensely successful missionary tours of Paul and Barnabas (and later Silas) there were many congregations that were started which were not fully organized. Nor were they mature enough to be. For that reason, Timothy and Titus found themselves doing some of the follow-up (mop-up) work to help bring those struggling congregations to the stage of maturity where they could select and ordain (with the laying on of the evangelists' hands) elders in every town (Titus 1:5) But, suffice it to say that was not the intended "work of an evangelist", but an expedient logistical necessity in the absence of any other qualified agent *to "set in order the things that are wanting"*. We observe from all this that the evangelist was not the, is not now, nor was he ever intended to be, an officer of the church sent to minister to the saints; but is rightly perceived as a messenger of Christ, ordained by the church and sent out from the church to the world...to bring to the world a message of good news.

Having now provided a biblical rationale and basis for our conclusions, we feel confident in describing the priorities, activities and accountabilities of the man we seek to fill the position of evangelist for our congregation. We seek a qualified individual who will:

1. Put the outreach program of xxxxxxxx as the top priority…the only priority of his ministry.
2. Define his role in that outreach as fully occupied with

    a. Personally taking that message himself to the homes of unbelievers.
    b. Training and equipping of other members of the body to participate in sharing their faith and winning the lost.
    c. Organizing these recruits into teams to create an army of Christian soldiers concerned enough about those without Christ to visit them in their homes, businesses, jails, social gatherings, or wherever the spirit wills that they go.
    d. Providing a mentor role for the inspiration and imitation of others in the body to follow in the activity of evangelism.

3. Use the worship assembly of the saints as a training ground for himself and other Christians to exhort one another and build one another up in the faith, not as a primary means of communicating the good news to the lost.

4. Recognize the administrative and pastoral prerogatives of the shepherds of the flock who are charged with the oversight, counseling, feeding and direction hereof.

We see the evangelist as a necessary piece of the puzzle which, when all parts are fitted together, comprise the picture of the New Testament Church.

Summary: At xxxxxxxxxxxxxxxxxx, we believe that God has precisely structured His church in order to make it the effective organization that He wants it to be. By adherence to the New Testament pattern, we believe that the 21st century church can become a dynamic, exciting, need-filling, soul-saving, praise-giving, spiritually-growing body of people. We are, therefore, pursuing a vision of the church that we see described in the pages of the New Testament.

This church, the church of our vision, is a church where the pastors/elders actually do shepherd the flock, and where their primary responsibility is the care, feeding and protection of the body of believers. The church of our vision has deacons who are servants to the body. It has members who, in their various stages of Christian maturity, feel the responsibility to use their gifts and become ministers, serving one another.

And, finally, but by no means the least, the church of our vision has an evangelist whose charge, and God-given responsibility is to take the "good news" to the world. We see the evangelist as being totally consumed with the desire and drive to win souls to Christ personally, to train and to organize the members of the congregation to become effective soul winners.

We do not see the evangelist as being preoccupied with the feeding, shepherding and nurturing of those who are already Christians. That's the work of the pastor/elders described above. The evangelist needs to spend his time on the lost, and not diffuse his energy by well-intentioned, though inappropriate, service to the body.

The practical implications of this division of labor may result in some situation which may be untraditional. For example, the evangelist may spend virtually no time in the church building, but may, in fact, maintain his office off-premises. This arrangement would discourage church members calling on the evangelist to perform administrative tasks, and help to keep him focused on the lost, not those already within the body. The implication here is that the evangelist must be strongly committed to his job—committed to the extend that he can say "no" when appropriate, and committed to the extent that he can withstand pressure to take on more traditional "pastoral" tasks.

Although evangelism is the responsibility of every Christian, with the evangelist evangelizing, the burden of responsibility to see to it that the body is shepherded falls on the pastors/elders. This is as it should be.

We believe that it's only when each of the individuals who function in the church do so according to God's pattern, will the church become the glorious organization God wants. The church that we envision.

ATTACHMENT 2

The Second of Our Organizational Documents:
A Position Paper

What Are the Responsibilities of the Elders?

What Are the Responsibilities of the Evangelist?

In the New Testament, there are three Greek words used to refer to the office we call "Elder". These are listed below:

Presbuteros—Those who presided over the assemblies. Those who managed public affairs and administered justice.

Acts 11:30; Acts 15:2, 4, 6, 22; Acts 20:17
Acts 21:18, Titus 1:5, II John 1
I Peter 5:1-5, Acts 14:23, Acts 16:4
I Tim. 5:17, I Tim. 5:19, III John 1

Poimen—A man to whose care and control others have committed themselves. The Presiding Officer, Manager, Director of any assembly.

Matt. 9:36, Matt. 25:32, Matt. 26:31
Eph 4:11, John 21:16, Acts 20:28
I Peter 5:2, Mark 6:34, Mark 14:27
Luke 2:8, 15, 18, 20; John 10:2, 12; John 10:11-14

Episcopus—A man charged with the duty of seeing that things to be done by others are done rightly.

Acts 20:28, Heb 13:17, I Peter 5:2
Phil 1:1, I Tim 3:2, Titus 1:7

That these three words all refer to one office can be seen by the fact that the words are used interchangeably in the New Testament. While there are several examples of these, two clear examples are Acts 20:28, and I Peter 5; 1-5.

> From Miletus, Paul sent to Ephesus for the elders (Presbuteros) of the church…Keep watch over yourselves and all the flock of which the Holy Spirit has made you overseers. (Episcopus) Be shepherds (Poimen) of the church of God.
>
> (Acts 20:17 & 28)

> To the elders (Presbuteros) among you…Be shepherds (Poimen) of God's flock that is under your care, serving as overseers (Episcopus).
>
> (I Peter 5:1 & 2)

There is, then, only one position, but three terms which highlight different facets of that position. While "Elder" is the most popular term today, any of the translations of any of the three words are equally appropriate: Shepherd, Manager, Overseer, Pastor, Bishop, Administrator.

It should be noted that, contrary to popular usage in some of the denominations, the Bible never used the word Poimen (Pastor) to refer to a paid staff position. The Pastors in the New Testament are always plural, and always refer to the men we call "elders". The whole denominational concept of "Pastor" as the individual who is responsible for the congregation is non-scriptural. J. W. McGarvey wrote a short piece in 1864 which captures the views commonly held by the xxxxxxxxxxxxxxxx churches:

> The term pastor furnishes a striking example of the power with which sectarian usage forces itself upon us. In former times, it was not known in our phraseology. This was not because the brethren were ignorant of its existence in the English Scriptures, but because the word has acquired, in popular usage, an unscriptural sense. We had no officer in our churches, and we read of none in the New Testament corresponding precisely to the modern pastor, and therefore, we had no use for the word in its popular currency. We were not compelled, indeed, to use the term at all, and therefore, we did not even search into its proper or scriptural usage. But now, it has gained a currency among us almost as universal as among the Presbyterians and Baptists, and in quite the same sense. We have had various attempts to reconcile this

usage with our practices and principles in other respects, all of which tend to its establishment as a fixture among us. In none of the essays having this purpose in view have we seen an attempt to trace out the exact New Testament sense of the term. On the contrary, the writers have completely ignored this first and most essential of all the means of preserving a pure speech and have gone on to dogmatize after the most approved sectarian method...Although this term occurs in the New Testament eighteen times, and is in every other instance rendered Shepherd. In seven of these instances, it is used literally for the man who attends a flock of sheep; in nine it is applied figuratively to Jesus, and in only one is it applied to a class of officers in the church. Now there is no good reason for a departure in this single instance from a rendering which would otherwise be uniform throughout the New Testament. (17)

What are the duties of these elders/pastors/overseers? There are two avenues to take to fully understand what God wanted to convey to us in this respect. First, look at the original Greek words and understand what they meant when used....What does a Manager (Presbuteros) do? Our Sunday School class said a manager:

1. Was responsible to a higher authority
2. Leads

3. Delegates authority and responsibility
4. Disciplines
5. Encourages
6. Develops the potential in himself and his charges
7. Makes decisions
8. Organizes

What does a shepherd/pastor do? Again, our class said:

1. Keeps watch
2. Protects the flock
3. Provides necessities
4. Cares for and loves the flock.

In the same way, an overseer:

1. Teaches and gives example
2. Sees to it that things are done rightly

Based just upon this word study, it's clear that the elders/pastors/overseers are to be the managers and protectors of the congregation, the individuals responsible to God for the flock. Is this understanding compatible with the specific guidelines given in scripture? The attached list from xxxxxxxxxxxxxxxxxxxxxxxxxxxxx captures these guidelines accurately.

A study of these scriptures makes it obvious that the elders/pastors/overseers have specific responsibilities entirely consistent with the meaning of the terms used to describe them.

Scripture	Example or Precept	Extension to Christ's Church
Acts 11:29-30	Represented the Jerusalem congregation in receiving an offering from others	Our elders shall represent our congregation before other Christians and other Christian groups or congregations.
Acts 15:1-29	Conferred with the apostles and others in settling a matter of dispute.	Our elders shall settle matters of dispute through conference and through study.
Acts 20:28	Feed the church of the Lord.	Our elders shall see to it that the spiritual hunger of the members of our congregation is well cared for and fed.
Acts 20:29-31	Protect and guard the church from "wolves", both inside and outside the church.	Our elders shall protect us from those who spread false doctrines, whether they be outsiders seeking to delude the saints, or members of the church.
Acts 20:35	Help the weak	Our elders shall see that those with physical or spiritual needs get adequate and necessary aid.
Acts 21:17-24	Advised Paul on how to allay false opposition	Our elders shall counsel staff ministers on handling internal and external turmoil and disputes.

Scripture	Example or Precept	Extension to Christ's Church
Ephesians 4:11-16	Equip the saints so the saints can do the work of ministry	Our elders shall know members' spiritual gifts and needs, and then equip our members so they can use their gifts in service to Christ.
I Thess. 5:12-13	Admonish and direct disciples	Our elders shall counsel, admonish, and discipline church members with personal, ethical, or spiritual problems.
I Timothy 3:2	Teach	Our elders shall teach.
I Timothy 5:17	Work at preaching and teaching	Our elders shall bring energy, time, and enthusiasm to the task of teaching the Word of god and persuading men and women to believe and obey it.
Titus 1:10-11	Exhort with sound doctrine and convict (silence) gainsayers	Our elders shall be able to refute dissenters and persuade all Christians to biblical positions with sound doctrine and discipline accordingly.
Hebrews 13:17	Watch on behalf of souls	Our elders shall be constantly sensitive to the spiritual direction our members are moving and they shall care for the ultimate salvation of each Christian.

Scripture	Example or Precept	Extension to Christ's Church
James 5:14-15	Pray for the sick	Our elders shall be depended upon for prayer and aid whenever and wherever the need arises.
I Peter 5:1-5	Set an example	Our elders shall demonstrate in their own personal example in what terms all Christians are to live and grow and walk, so that each member may emulate and imitate their own spiritual pilgrimage.
Other scriptural titles for elders imply other responsibilities as follows:		
Overseer (episkopoi)		Our elders shall engage in directive work and wisdom in church affairs
Shepherd (poimenes)		Our elders shall be protectors and concerned caretakers
Leaders (egumenoi)		Our elders shall be guides and leaders
Superintendent (oikonomon)		Our elders shall administrate the spiritual meeting of members' needs
Teachers (didaskoloi)		Our elders shall impart knowledge and understanding

Reflect on these scriptures and several generalizations become apparent:

1. Very clearly, the elders/pastors/overseers are charged with the leadership responsibilities for the congregation.
2. The responsibilities of the elders/pastors/overseers are always the responsibilities of the group, not the individual. There is to be no "predominant" elder, but rather they are to function together, as a unit. Additionally, they are always referred to in plural, so that there must be more than one elder/pastor/oversee. The idea that one individual can raise himself up as the pastor is, perhaps, as example of the apostasy that Paul warned about in Acts 20:17-28.
3. The responsibilities of the elders/pastors/overseers are related to the local body and the individual believers. The implication here is that the elders/pastors/overseers have enough to do in leading and overseeing the body to spend much time on those outside the body, and that they ought not to diffuse their time and energy and thus short-change the believers and neglect their duties to the congregation.

What about the Evangelist? What are his duties? Again, let's look at the meaning of the Greek word. "Evangelist" is a transliteration of the Greed word which means "Good News". An Evangelist, literally, a "Good Newser", a teller of the good news about Jesus. The implication is that an Evangelist ought to be someone who tells others about the Good News, and who does it better and more often than those Christians who are not "Good Newsers". The specific guidelines in scripture are entirely consistent with this understanding. These directions to the evangelists, Timothy and Titus, give us an excellent picture of the responsibilities of the evangelist:

I Timothy

1:13 command...not to teach
1:19 hold unto the faith...
4:6   point these things out...
4:7   train yourself to be Godly...
4:11 command...teach
4:12 set an example
4:13 devote yourself to public reading of scripture... preaching and teaching
4:15 be diligent...give yourself wholly
4:15 exhort
4:16 watch your life and doctrine
4:17 persevere in them
5:13 give proper recognition to widows
5:19 do not entertain an accusation
5:21 keep these instructions without partiality
6:11 pursue righteousness, godliness, faith, love, endurance, gentleness
6:12 fight the good fight
6:14 keep the commandment
6:20 guard what has been entrusted

Titus

1:5   appoint elders
1:13 rebuke rebellious people
2:1   teach "sound doctrine"
2:7   show integrity, seriousness, soundness of speech
2:8   be an example
2:15 encourage and rebuke
3:1   remind…
3:10 warn…

II Timothy

1:6   fan into flames the gift of God
1:8   join in suffering
1:13 keep the pattern
1:14 guard the good deposit
2:1   be strong
2:2   entrust to reliable men
2:7   reflect
2:14 warn them
2:15 do your best to present yourself
2:16 avoid godless chatter
2:22 flee evil…pursue righteousness
2:25 gently instruct
2:23 don't have anything to do with foolish arguments
2:24 do not quarrel…be kind
3:14 continue in what you have learned
4:1   preach the Word
4:2   correct, rebuke, encourage
4:5   keep your head

4:5   endure hardship
4:5   do the work of an evangelist

Reflect on these directions and it becomes apparent that they fall into two broad categories, giving us a picture of the two-sided responsibilities of the evangelist. First, is the responsibility to grow in knowledge of God's Word and to grow in individual spirituality. These directions, having to do with the evangelists relationship to God's Word and his own spiritual growth are represented in, among others: Titus 2:8, 2:7, I Timothy 1:19, 4:7, 4:12, etc.

Most of the specific directions to evangelists refer, however, to the Evangelist's duty to preach and teach God's Word to all the people. See I Timothy 4:13, 4:15, II Timothy 25:25, 4:1, Titus 2:1, 2:15, etc.

All of this is entirely consistent with the understanding of the work of the Evangelist as a "Good Newser", a proclaimer, by his life and by his preaching and teaching, of God's Word.

It is interesting to compare and contrast the directions and focus for the evangelist with those of the pastors. The evangelist's responsibility is directed to the proclaiming of god's Word to people both in and out of the body. The enders/pastors/overseers and the evangelist have been directed to "refute dissenters", and to teach and preach. Again, the elders are responsible for that activity within the body, the evangelist both within and without. Both are directed to be examples, and to "guard". But note that the elder/pastor/overseers are to "guard the flock", while the evangelist is directed to "guard the pattern", "that which has been entrusted".

Noticeably lacking from directions to the evangelist are directions having to do with "overseeing, managing, leading, administering, shepherding, or pasturing, etc." Instead, the evangelist is told to "devote yourself" (I Timothy 4:13), and "give yourself wholly" (I Timothy 4:15) to the work of an evangelist. The two exceptions to this are the directions regarding widows (I Timothy 5:3) and the instructions "to appoint elders". I believe both of these have to do with the evangelists' duty to preach the Word to the world. The natural result is a body of believers who need to be taught and directed until such time as elders/pastors/overseers arise. The evangelist is to "finish" his work by appointing elders/pastors/overseers.

It is interesting to note that just as directions to evangelize outside the body are noticeably lacking from the responsibilities of the elders/pastors/overseers, so directions to manage and lead those inside the body are noticeable lacking from the direction to the evangelist. It appears that the Lord intended for there to be a separation of responsibilities.

The diagram below is an attempt to graphically portray scripture's direction:

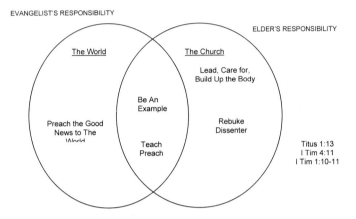

EVANGELIST'S RESPONSIBILITY

ELDER'S RESPONSIBILITY

The World

The Church

Lead, Care for,
Build Up the Body

Be An
Example

Preach the Good
News to The
World

Rebuke
Dissenter

Teach
Preach

Titus 1:13
I Tim 4:11
I Tim 1:10-11

Often, evangelists are called "ministers". Is this scriptural? The word "minister" is a translation of the Greek word "Diakonos". Its meaning is, simply, "servant". From this word comes the transliteration, "Deacon". While scripture gives qualifications for the office of "Deacon", it give no responsibilities. So what is a "Deacon" to do? Whatever the elders, who are the organizers and leaders of the congregation, have for them to do.

While a deacon holds a formal office, any Christian can be a servant or minister, by performing a service or ministry for the Lord. As servants of the church, these ministers are also under the authority of the elders/pastors/overseers. A paid staff member may, therefore, be a minister or servant, under the authority of the eldership, in the same way that any believer can be.

What should be the relationship between the elders and the evangelist? I believe that in God's plan, as the evangelist goes about his work, he develops a body of believers. During this phase of the growth of the church, the evangelist often functions as a "pastor" because of the lack of mature Christian men, and because of the credibility attached to the evangelist's greater knowledge of the Word.

However, as the congregation matures, it develops elders/pastors/ overseers who are then put in place as the leaders of the congregation. The evangelist must, in keeping with God's word, pass any perceived and/ or real authority he has over to the elders. The evangelist may then remain with the congregation for a time, as Paul did at Ephesus, or move on, as Titus and Timothy did.

While he remains in the congregation, I believe the evangelist is subject to God only in respect to his personal spiritual growth, and in respect to his responsibility to preach and teach those outside the body. As a member of the congregation, however, he needs to acknowledge the oversight of the elders, just as any other member.

How does all this relate to xxxxxxxx church today? I believe that the bible knows no position like that often called "pastor" or "minister" in today's church. However, the principles discussed above can be applied to help sort through some of the situations which have developed as tradition, rather than out of study of scripture.

In a situation where there are elders/pastors/overseers, and they deem it advisable to pay a full-time staff member, that member may be delegated "ministry", or may be an evangelist, or may be a combination of the two. There the elders/pastor/overseers have elected to support an evangelist, preaching and teaching, especially to the lost. While the elders may want to avail themselves of his counsel, that individual should have no authority over the congregation. Since he accepts financial support from the eldership, he should be accountable to them for this stewardship of his ministry.

If the elders choose to delegate certain of their responsibilities to him, then he should be accountable to them for these ministries, just as anyone to whom duties are delegated should be.

Is the evangelist automatically an elder? There is certainly no scripture that would indicate this. In addition, a comprehensive look at the duties and responsibilities of both the elders and the evangelist indicates that the two are separate functions. God intended the evangelist to remain free of the responsibilities of the elders, and to stay away from the temptations to become weighted down with tasks outside his area of responsibility. Timothy wasn't told to devote himself to his work and to someone else's. He was told to do the work of an evangelist. He was not told to do the work of an evangelist and the work of the elders. I believe this separation of function and responsibility of God's plan. To do anything other is to raise ourselves up as being wiser than God.

While this separation of function and responsibility should preclude an evangelist from being an elder, it does not preclude a paid staff "minister, who is not an evangelist, and who is qualified to be an elder, from becoming one. This individual, like any member of the church, may go through the same process of selection and appointment that any other member would go through.

Attachment 3

The Third of Our Organizational Documents: A Job Description for the Evangelist

Job Description

Employing Institution: XXXXXXXXXXXX
(Herein after referred to as "the church")

Job Title: Evangelist

Reports to: Elders of the Church

In fulfillment of the scriptural duties of the evangelist, the brother engaged by the church for that divine and sacred role will be responsible for:

1. Heading up the outreach program of the church. This includes:

   - Calling on non-Christians and those without current church commitments
   - Recruiting members of the local body to be trained in personal evangelism
   - Implementing calling programs for those thus trained to go out two-by-two.

2. Providing the exhortation at regularly scheduled/ appointed worship assemblies of the church.

3. Assisting in the development of new potential candidates for elders and deacons, resulting in the ordination of those thus qualified.
4. Working with the shepherds/elders of the church to coordinate membership visitation, counseling, hospital ministry, and church growth.
5. Minimal administrative duties will be required due to the church retaining a professional staff administrator.

NOTE: Performance of all above duties are under the leadership and authority of the shepherds/elders/bishops of the church.

ATTACHMENT 4

The Fourth of Our Organizational Documents: Long Range Strategic Plan

Objective 1: Worship

The evangelist worships with the church the same as other members of the body.

He participates in the exhortation of the assembled saints and just as regularly participates in equipping others for the same ministry.

He may bring special music, serve at the table, lead singing, offer prayers, act as worship leader to the same degree, but not more than, nor less than, any other active, responsible member of the body.

Inasmuch as the exhortation portion of the worship assembly is directed at believing brothers and sisters in

Christ, it is expected that the content will primarily be to admonish to holiness and service as outlined in the apostle's doctrine. This may be focused at areas of need as observed and directed by the shepherds of the flock.

Objective 2: Administration

No involvement is anticipated by the evangelist with church programs, other than evangelism and equipping, over and above that expected of any other member.

No time in the church office other than the necessary communication requirements that pertain to the execution of the evangelism, equipping and exhortation responsibilities with which he is directly concerned.

The church will retain a professional clerical staff to accommodate the requirements of the daily administration.

Objective 3: Evangelism

The evangelist is responsible for heading up the outreach program of the church. This includes:

- Calling on non-Christians and those without current church commitments
- Recruiting members of the church to be trained in personal evangelism
- Implementing calling programs for those thus trained to go out two-by-two.

Objective 4: Shepherding

No shepherding or ministering to the saints more than, nor less than, any other Christian is expected.

Objective 5: Education Program/
Teaching Responsibilities

It is not the responsibility of the evangelist to conduct classes at the regularly appointed learning sessions of the church. He will attend as a co-learner and a vitally interested student. No responsibility above and beyond that expected of any other Christian.

Objective 6: Relationships

A. Relationship with the elders—the evangelist will be in subjection to their authority. He will give cheerful deference in matters of church doctrine and discipline.
B. He will overtly demonstrate respect for the elders and avoid any appearance of rebuking them before others.
C. Relationship with the church—the evangelist as a loving brother to all other Christians will be sensitive to their needs for dignity, self-respect and hurts. He has no authority or responsibilities relative to the body more than, nor less than, other members of the church.

D. Self-development, as it relates to the physical, intellectual and spiritual:

- Physical—should have a program of health and lifestyle for the optimum utilization of the temple of the Holy Spirit.
- Intellectual—additional education is advantageous for mental stimulation and refreshment.
- Spiritual—use retreat type experiences for inner growth.

The evangelist has at least the same responsibility to develop in these areas of self-improvement as any other Christian. The elders expect and encourage the evangelist, because of this very visible role as a representative of the congregation, to pro-actively develop in these areas perhaps over and above the average/norm.

A PERSONAL NOTE
FROM THE AUTHOR

The most common response I hear from people who read this book goes something like this: *"I've thought a lot of these same things myself, but I've been afraid to mention them to anyone."*

The paradigms which prevent our talking about these issues and inhibit us from even asking the questions are incredibly strong and have hindered the Spirit among us for too long. Help break though those paradigms and create a climate where these questions can be asked and these ideas discussed.

Here are four things you can do.

1. Subscribe to our Ezine, "A Call to Arms." http://www.acalltoarms.co/
2. Buy multiple copies of this book, and give them away to your friends and associates.
3. Recommend this book to your friends and associates.
4. Pray that the Lord would multiply the distribution of this book.

Thanks,
Dave Kahle

ABOUT THE AUTHOR

Dave came to Christ at age twenty-four after a period of searching following a Catholic upbringing. He and his wife, Coleen, have raised five children and been foster parents to nineteen foster children. He's been a Bible teacher, an elder, a house church leader, and a short-term missionary. For thirty years, he has made a living as an internationally recognized authority in sales and sales systems. In that regard, he has written ten books which have been translated into eight languages and are available in at least twenty countries and presented in forty-seven states and ten countries. In addition, he is a chapter president for Truth@Work Christian Business Roundtables and facilitates both local and virtual executive meetings. He and Coleen split their time between Sarasota, Florida, and Grand Rapids, Michigan.

You can contact him at www.davekahle.com.

You can review other books by Dave Kahle here: http://www.acalltoarms.co/books/

Sign up for his "Call to Arms" Ezine here: http://www.acalltoarms.co/

NOTES

1. We've Lost the Culture
   Hillman, Os, *Faith & Work*, an EBook by Os Hillman, p. 31, Marketplace Leaders.
2. Enlow, Johnny, *The Seven Mountain Prophecy,* by Johnny Enlow. Creation House, 2008.
3. Habash, Gabe, *The Bestselling Books of 2012* in Publishers' Weekly, *Top of the Charts*, by Gabe Habash, Jan. 04, 2013.
4. According to the National Center for Educational Statistics' Indicators of School Crimes Safety 2009 report, "For the first time, rates of violent crime victimization at school were higher than rates of violent crime victimization away from school. In 2007, there were 26 violent crimes per 1,000 students at school, compared to 20 violent crimes per 1,000 students away from school."
   Gunn, Colin; Fernandez, Joaquin, *IndoctriNation* (Kindle Locations 486-489). (2012-08-29). Master Books. Kindle Edition.
5. The number of cohabiting unmarried partners increased by 88% between 1990 and 2007 (CPS 2007).

http://www.unmarried.org/press-room/briefing-kit/.

6. Jayson, Sharon, *'First Union' now more likely to be cohabitation"*, USA Today, Thursday, April 4, 2013, p. 8A.

7. Baker, Jennifer, Forest Institute of Professional Psychology, "Fifty (50%) percent of first marriages, 67% of second and 74% of third marriages end in divorce", Springfield, Missouri. http://www.divorcerate.org/

8. Kinnaman, Dave and Lyone, Gabe, *unChristian*, p. 127 Baker Books, 2007.

9. Gunn, Colin and Fernandez, Joaquin *IndoctriNation* (Kindle Locations 627-630). (2012-08-29). Master Books. Kindle Edition.

10. And That's Not All
Kinnaman, David, p. 27. Baker Books, 2011.

11. Kinnaman, David and Lyone, Gabe, *unChristian*, pgs. 47, 74, 77 and 142, Baker Books, 2007.

12. unChristian, by David Kinnaman and Gabe Lyone, p. 47, Baker Books, 2007.

13. unChristian, by David Kinnaman and Gabe Lyone, p. 47, Baker Books, 2007.

14. unChristian, by David Kinnaman and Gabe Lyone, p. 74, Baker Books, 2007.

15. unChristian, by David Kinnaman and Gabe Lyone, p. 77, Baker Books, 2007.

16. It's Our Fault

> [6]*But you have this in your favor: You hate the practices of the Nicolaitans, which I also hate.* [15] *Like-*

*wise, you also have those who hold to the teaching
of the Nicolaitans.*

(Revelation 2:6, 15)

17. Where the Church Went Wrong
Barna, George and Viola, Frank, *Pagan Christianity*,
Barna Books, 2008.

18. McGarvey, J. W. Quote attributed to J.W.
McGarvey, a writer/teacher who was part of
the movement to restore the church to New
Testament practices. See the websites http://
onlinebooks.library.upenn.edu/webbin/book/
lookupname?key=McGarvey%2C%20J.%20W.%20
%28John%20William%29%2C%201829-1911 and
http://www.christianlibrary.org/authors/J_W_
McGarvey/JW_McGarvey.htm for more of
his writing.

19. Beyond the Biblical Case—Practical Implications
How many denominations are there? http://wiki.
answers.com/Q/How_many_Christian_denomina-
tions_are_there

20. But That's Not All
Rutz, James H., *The Open Church*, The Seed Sowers,
1992

21. Barna, George and Viola, Frank, *Pagan Christianity,*
Barna Books, 2008.

22. God's Majestic Church
How many Christians in China? http://www.billion-
bibles.org/china/how-many-christians-in-china.
html

23. Barna, George, *How Many People Really Attend a House Church?* George Barna Group http://www.barna.org/organic-church-articles/291-how-many-people-really-attend-a-house-church-barna-study-finds-it-depends-on-the-definition

24. Hillman, Os. TGIF website (Today God is First) http://www.crosswalk.com/devotionals/market-place/.